# BEYOND THE PLATE

INCLUDES
60 RECIPES

# BEYOND
# THE PLATE

© Prestel Verlag, Munich · London · New York 2017
A member of Verlagsgruppe Random House GmbH
Neumarkter Strasse 28 · 81673 Munich

In respect to links in the book, Verlagsgruppe Random House expressly notes that no illegal content was discernible on the linked sites at the time the links were created. The Publisher has no influence at all over the current and future design, content or authorship of the linked sites. For this reason Verlagsgruppe Random House expressly disassociates itself from all content on linked sites that has been altered since the link was created and assumes no liability for such content.

Text © 2017 Daniela Galarza
Foreword text © 2017 Adam Sachs

Prestel Publishing Ltd.
14-17 Wells Street
London W1T 3PD

Prestel Publishing
900 Broadway, Suite 603
New York, NY 10003

Library of Congress Cataloging-in-Publication Data

Names: Sachs, Adam, writer of foreword. | Galarza, Daniela.
Title: Beyond the plate : top food blogs from around the world / foreword by
   Adam Sachs ; text by Daniela Galarza.
Description: Munich ; New York : Prestel, [2017] | Includes index.
Identifiers: LCCN 2016037475 | ISBN 9783791382777
Subjects: LCSH: Cooks. | Cooking—Blogs. | Food—Blogs. | LCGFT: Cookbooks.
Classification: LCC TX649.A1 B49 2016 | DDC 641.5092--dc23
LC record available at https://lccn.loc.gov/2016037475

A CIP catalogue record for this book is available from the British Library.

Editorial direction: Holly La Due
Design and layout: Amy Sly
Production: Luke Chase
Copyediting: Lauren Salkeld, John Son
Proofreading: Monica Parcell
Index: Marilyn Bliss

Photography Credits
Front cover: My Darling Lemon Thyme
Previous spread: Southern Soufflé
Opposite: Indian Simmer
Page 8: Feed Me Phoebe
Page 11: My Daily Sourdough Bread
Pages 12–13: Sassy Kitchen
Back cover: Chocolate + Marrow (top), Krautkopf (bottom left), and Anett Velsberg (bottom right)

MIX
Paper from
responsible sources
FSC® C008047
www.fsc.org

Verlagsgruppe Random House FSC® N001967
Printed on the FSC®-certified paper Chinese Hoopoe woodfree FSC

Printed in China

ISBN 978-3-7913-8277-7

www.prestel.com

**Anett Velsberg** 14

**Bottom of the Pot** 20

**Broad Appetite** 26

**Cannelle et Vanille** 32

**Chocolate + Marrow** 38

**The Clever Carrot** 44

**Eat In My Kitchen** 50

**Feed Me Phoebe** 56

**The Food Gays** 62

**Hortus Cuisine** 68

**I Will Not Eat Oysters** 74

**Indian Simmer** 80

**Kaluhi's Kitchen** 86

**Krautkopf** 92

**Lab Noon** 98

**Lady and Pups** 104

**Local Milk** 110

**My Daily Sourdough Bread** 116

**My Darling Lemon Thyme** 124

**No Gojis, No Glory** 130

**Pastry Affair** 136

**Ren Behan** 142

**Renée Kemps** 148

**Sassy Kitchen** 154

**Southern Soufflé** 160

**This Rawsome Vegan Life** 166

**Three Little Halves** 172

**Twigg Studios** 178

**The Woks of Life** 184

**Vanelja** 190

# FOREWORD

BY Adam Sachs

Did someone break it to *The Food Gays*? Has word reached *My Darling Lemon Thyme* in New Zealand? Surely Christine at *No Gojis, No Glory* and the entire *Wok of Life* crew—Bill, Judy, Sarah and Kaitlin—have all been apprised of the news?

Blogging's dead, didn't you hear? Especially food blogging—that benign blip of a media moment, that sweet and outmoded thing where suddenly you didn't need to have a big book deal or a column at a glossy magazine to share your recipes and tell your food story. Food blogging's been eclipsed by the oversharing onslaught of the Instagram age. Nobody needs a blog when you can post everything you eat in real time. So the bloggers moved on and so did their loyal readers.

Except, of course, they didn't really and neither did we.

At *Saveur* we tallied 30,000 nominations for our 7th annual Blog Awards. In 2015 we welcomed finalists and winners from across the US as well as Ireland, Australia—and one from Slovenia focused entirely on sourdough bread. In 2016, in addition to the usual nods for new and established compelling voices across travel, recipe, drink, video, health, and style categories, we gave out our first-ever Golden Biscuit Award which recognizes a blog that's been in business for ten or more years.

Think about that for a moment: A running, intimate, food-fueled conversation that spans a decade. It's an impressive feat for any form and one for which conversations about what and how and why and where we eat is uniquely well suited since it's a topic that keeps us curious and hungry, informed and inspired. Far from being outmoded by social sharing and the apps that encourage it, food blogging has established itself as an enduring medium for people who really care and think about what they're cooking—for family, for friends, for themselves—to reach a curious, engaged audience. Some authors go into it with a business model and a dream, while most are in it mainly for this connection.

I like to think of *Saveur*, its staff and readers, as a community of culinary enthusiasts. Food bloggers are our tribe.

We see their passion when we get them in a room to celebrate our Blog Awards. And we see their continued reach and impact in the way they help shape the culinary conversation and aesthetics of traditional food media. And we see it on our bookshelves as members of this largely self-trained army of writers, stylists, bakers, photographers, and storytellers publish their own cookbooks and make it into a lovely collection like the one you're holding in your hands now. So here's to the amateurs out there who make food writing less staid, homogenous, and dull, who wisely ignored the premature notices of the untimely passing of a favorite form, who keep us hooked and cooking and amused with their tireless dispatches from their many kitchens. Long live the food blog!

# INTRODUCTION

BY Daniela Galarza

Thousands of food blogs live on the web, from Alaska to Azerbaijan, Nairobi to North Ireland, and Vietnam to Venezuela. Voices with marked acumen in photography, food styling, and recipe development overflow with passion for food, travel, and the culture of cuisine. Sifting through hundreds of them was humbling, but also led to self-questioning: *Why can't I do this?! What have I been doing with my life?* Like frosting a cake, running a successful food blog takes a steady hand. Like raising a child, it requires a full heart. It also demands an eye for design, web-specific aesthetics, and pleasing prose. With these guidelines in mind, we've chosen what we firmly believe are the best new food blogs from across the globe. These bloggers hail from countries far and wide, and many have lived in multiple cities and travel often. Some have won awards for their work, and at least half now blog full-time. Others are not as well known but no less passionate. To be clear, these are not the best food blogs on the Web. They are the most promising, and most are fewer than five years old.

The term blog was invented in the late 1990s, and though they were once often mundane accounts of daily life, cultural niches emerged. Recipe blogs were one of many categories to find an audience right away, booming in the early 2000s. The technology sector faced unprecedented boons and bloggers scrambled to find their way to monetize their work. After the tech bubble burst, food bloggers went back to basics—and there is nothing more basic than the daily meal. Soon we were graced with blogs like *Smitten Kitchen*, in which Deb Perelman learned to cook out of a tiny New York City kitchen; *Orangette*, which gave Molly Wizenberg a platform for her winding, dreamy prose; and *Chocolate and Zucchini*, where Clotilde Dusoulier found a voice for her Parisian and internationally inspired cookery.

Today's top bloggers have their own TV shows, and an endless stream of cookbooks was born out of the Internet. Here's the next class of food bloggers. We trust they'll go on to do great things and create tantalizing recipes for years to come.

THE RECIPES

ANETT
VELSBERG

# Anett Velsberg

Cape Town, South Africa
www.anettvelsberg.com

Anett Velsberg's eponymous blog highlights her life as a food photographer, stylist, and recipe developer. Though she currently lives in Cape Town, South Africa, she's originally from Estonia. Every week—sometimes more often—Velsberg shares a recipe inspired by home or by her travels. The recipes lean on health-forward ingredients, including tofu, green tea, miso, chia seeds, and kimchi, though Velsberg often indulges in recipes for sweets like Cinnamon, Maple, and Blueberry Rolls, Roasted Strawberry Doughnuts with Tellicherry Pepper, and Miso Caramel Dark Chocolate Cups (a mouthful in text and mouth!). Velsberg experiments with alternative flours, grains, and milks. Her recipe introductions are brief and to-the-point; recipes themselves include clear instructions and useful tips. But it's Velsberg's photography, with its vibrant colors, intense sharpness, and depth of field that make reading her blog akin to reading a magazine or book. Immersive and exploratory, she has a knack for capturing a food's best side, be it a grilled cheese sandwich, a just-cut brownie, or a stack of spinach pancakes. The photograph of a Peach and Thyme Galette on a Rye Flour Base makes the peaches look like they're dancing atop a ribboned petticoat. Mango and Berry Layered Smoothies look like sand art in a jar, and a Kimchi Rice Bowl contains every color of the rainbow. Behind the glossy images Velsberg reveals herself to be that cool girl everyone wants as their best friend.

## Q+A

**What is the most treasured item in your kitchen?**
My grandmother's blue-and-white linen kitchen towel.

**What is your ultimate comfort food?**
A brioche lobster roll.

**Name a utensil you can't live without.**
My Santoku knife.

**What is your go-to breakfast?**
Savory almond milk oatmeal with avocado and toasted nuts.

**What is your go-to cocktail?**
Tom Collins, extra lemon juice!

**Who is your culinary idol?**
René Redzepi and Massimo Bottura.

SERVES
3 TO 4

# THAI RED CURRY NOODLE SOUP

## INGREDIENTS

4 tablespoons vegetable oil

2 large cloves garlic, finely chopped

1 shallot, finely chopped

1 inch (2.5 cm) piece fresh ginger, finely grated

1 stalk lemongrass, finely chopped with tough outer layer removed

½ teaspoon ground coriander

½ teaspoon ground cumin

3¼ cups (750 ml) vegetable stock

1¾ cups (400 ml) coconut cream

4 tablespoons Thai red curry paste

Juice of ½ to 1 lime

Soy sauce

Salt

Ground pepper

3½ ounces (100 g) shiitake mushrooms, thinly sliced (about 4 mushrooms)

7 ounces (200 g) broccolini or broccoli, roughly chopped

1 (200 g) package thin rice noodles

2 cups (500 ml) boiling water

1 small handful fresh cilantro leaves

Sesame seeds

## METHOD

In a medium pot, heat 2 tablespoons vegetable oil over medium-high heat. Add the garlic, shallot, ginger, lemongrass, coriander, and cumin and sauté for 3 minutes or until fragrant. Add the vegetable stock and bring to a boil. Reduce the heat and simmer for 15 minutes. Add the coconut cream and curry paste, stir well, and simmer for another 5 to 10 minutes or until the broth is well infused with the flavors. Season to taste with lime juice, soy sauce, salt, and pepper.

While the broth is simmering, cook the vegetables: In a medium pan, heat the remaining 2 tablespoons vegetable oil over medium-high heat. Add the shiitakes and sauté for 3 to 5 minutes or until golden, then stir in a tablespoon of water to soften and season to taste with lime juice and soy sauce. Transfer the shiitakes to a bowl and set aside. Place the pan back over medium heat, add the broccolini or broccoli, and sauté for 3 to 5 minutes or until tender but still a bit crunchy, adding a splash of water to speed up the process if you like. Season to taste with salt and pepper.

Place the rice noodles in a large bowl. Add enough boiling water to completely submerge the noodles. Let sit, stirring every few minutes, for 5 to 7 minutes or until the noodles are softened.

To serve, divide the rice noodles among bowls, add the shiitakes and broccolini or broccoli, and top with the broth. Garnish with fresh cilantro and sesame seeds and serve immediately.

*Rich and hot, spicy and sour, with springy noodles, crunchy broccoli, and meaty shiitakes, this recipe delivers everything you want from a bowl of soup. Plus, it takes just half an hour to pull together.*

# CHOCOLATE, PEAR, AND HAZELNUT BUNS

MAKES 8 TO 10 BUNS

## METHOD

For the dough, in a large bowl, whisk together the chickpea flour and water. Add the almond milk, sugar, vegetable oil, yeast, and salt. Add the cake flour, a little at a time, and stir with a wooden spoon to bring the dough together. If the dough is sticky, add more flour, 1 tablespoon at a time, then turn out onto a lightly floured table or countertop. Knead for 5 minutes. Place the dough in a lightly oiled bowl, cover with plastic wrap, and let rise in a warm place for 1 hour or until doubled in size.

When the dough is ready, start prepping the filling: In a large heat-proof bowl set over a saucepan of barely simmering water, melt the chocolate and coconut oil.

Preheat the oven to 400°F (200°C). Line a baking sheet with parchment paper.

Lightly flour a large table or countertop and use a rolling pin to roll out the dough into a roughly 8 x 16-inch (20 x 40 cm) rectangle. Carefully transfer the dough to an unlined baking sheet, spread the melted chocolate all over and sprinkle the hazelnuts and grated pear on top of the chocolate. Place in the fridge for 10 minutes to harden the chocolate. Visually divide the dough lengthwise into thirds. Fold one third over the middle then fold the other third over the middle to meet the other side, as if you were folding a business letter. Use a rolling pin to carefully roll out the folded dough into a roughly 8 x 12-inch (20 cm x 30 cm) rectangle. Cut the rectangle lengthwise into 8 to 10 (¾-inch/2 cm) strips. Twist each strip of dough into an individual spiral. Then, to make the knots, wrap one strip around your hand twice, bringing the remaining length over the middle of the knot and tucking it underneath. Repeat with the remaining dough.

Arrange the buns on the lined baking sheet and brush with warmed maple syrup. Bake for 20 to 25 minutes or until golden. Let cool for a few minutes and enjoy warm or at room temperature.

## INGREDIENTS

*For the dough*

¼ cup (20 g) chickpea flour

3½ tablespoons water

¾ cup plus 2 tablespoons (200 ml) almond milk, lukewarm

4 tablespoons sugar

3½ tablespoons vegetable oil

2½ teaspoons instant yeast

¼ teaspoon salt

3¼ cups (350 g) unbleached cake flour, plus more for dusting

*For the fillings*

3 ounces (80 g) dark chocolate, finely chopped

1 tablespoon coconut oil

⅓ cup (50 g) hazelnuts, roughly chopped

2 medium unpeeled pears, cored, halved, and roughly grated with a medium-sized grater

Maple syrup, warmed

*Chocolaty, moist, and crunchy—these buns are the ultimate blend of traditional babka and Swedish cinnamon knots. The aroma that fills the kitchen as they bake is to die for!*

A specialty of the casual or formal Persian dinner table is *tahdig*, a buttery, crisp layer of caramelized rice. Sometimes potatoes or thin pieces of lavash bread are embedded in this lacy layer, adding texture to the crisp rice. And it is this gem of a dish that inspires the name of Naz Deravian's blog, *Bottom of the Pot*. Deravian lives with her husband and two children in Los Angeles, but arrived by way of Tehran, Rome, and Vancouver. These varied climates and cultures inform her cooking style, which is heavily influenced by Persian spices and floral herbs but can be casual like Roman antipasti. The photos on *Bottom of the Pot* are lush, but it's the poetic prose that brings this blog—and Deravian's family story—to life. Recipe introductions are broken up by conversations with her mother, her children, or a memory of someone she knew long ago. These memories add spice to her clear, straightforward descriptions. A recipe for chocolate yogurt pots is preceded by a conversation between Deravian and her husband about their children growing up too fast. A recipe for Persian marzipan involves a playful exchange between Deravian and her daughters, an almost stream of consciousness poem in which they celebrate the New Year (*Nowruz*) with sugar and cardamom and vibrant greens. Not just a recipe developer or photographer, Deravian is a poet and reading her tales on a lazy weekend afternoon will fill your mind with dreams of jeweled rice and crisp—always crisp—crunchy rice from the bottom of the pot.

# Bottom of the Pot

**Naz Deravian**
Los Angeles, California, United States
www.bottomofthepot.com

---

## Q+A

**What is the most treasured item in your kitchen?**
My tiny jar for saffron.

**What is your ultimate comfort food?**
Iranian saffron steamed rice, with a side of plain yogurt, and crunchy tahdig.

**What is your go-to breakfast?**
Green tea with almond butter toast or Persian black tea with feta cheese, barbari bread, and a side of watermelon.

**What is your go-to cocktail?**
Campari and Soda—forever and always!

**Who would you love to cook for?**
My children would really love me to cook for President Obama and his family. If Manu Chao and his band could also be in attendance then it would be grand.

**Name a utensil you can't live without.**
My Persian rice cooker.

# BOTTOM OF THE POT

## READER FAVORITE

# ZERESHK POLO (BARBERRY RICE)

## INGREDIENTS

3 cups (550 g) white basmati rice, rinsed

2 cups (480 ml) cold water

Fine sea salt

¼ teaspoon ground saffron, plus a small pinch

2 tablespoons hot water

6 tablespoons (90 g) unsalted butter

2 large onions, finely sliced

2 cups (140 g) dried barberries, soaked in cold water for 15 minutes, drained

1 tablespoon granulated sugar

3 tablespoons olive oil, plus more as needed

8 skinless, boneless chicken thighs

¼ teaspoon ground pepper

¼ cup kosher salt

## METHOD

In a large bowl, combine the rice with the cold water and 3 tablespoons sea salt; soak for 1 hour.

In a small bowl, steep the ¼ teaspoon saffron in the hot water for 5 minutes.

In a medium pan, melt 3 tablespoons (45 g) of the butter over medium heat. Add ¾ of the sliced onion, increase the heat to medium-high and sauté, stirring often, for 10 minutes or until golden. Reduce the heat to medium-low, sprinkle with a pinch of sea salt, and sauté for 30 minutes or until caramelized. Add the drained barberries, along with the sugar, stir to combine, and cook for 3 to 5 minutes or until the barberries are heated through and tender. Set aside.

While the onions caramelize, cook the chicken: Heat the oil in a large pot over medium heat. Scatter the remaining sliced onions in one layer on top of the oil. Place the chicken on top of the onion, season with 2 teaspoons sea salt, the pepper, and the saffron-infused water. Cover and bring to a simmer. Reduce the heat to low and simmer for 30 minutes or until the chicken is cooked through and tender. Transfer the chicken to a cutting board, cut into ½-inch sized pieces lengthwise, then return to the pan to rest in the juices.

In a separate large pot, combine 14 cups (3.3 l) water with the kosher salt and bring to a boil. Drain the rice, add it to the pot, and stir once. Return to a gentle boil, skimming off any foam, and cook the rice for 4 to 6 minutes or until al dente. Drain the rice then quickly and gently rinse it under cold running water. Leave to drain completely.

In a large nonstick pot, melt the remaining 3 tablespoons (45 g) butter over low heat. Add a very small pinch of saffron and swirl the pan. Add enough of the cooked rice to fully cover the bottom of the pot. Add another layer of rice, followed by a layer of the barberry-onion mixture, another layer of rice, and a layer of chicken, reserving the juices in the pan.

*Zereshk polo is quintessential Iranian home cooking—a feast for the senses and comfort food at its best. Enjoy this dish with a side of fresh green herbs (such as fresh basil and mint), yogurt-cucumber dip, and of course, tahdig, the crispy rice at the bottom of the pot.*

Continue adding alternating layers, about 2 spatulas of each depending on the size of your pot, gradually creating a pyramid shape and ending with a top layer of rice. Gently pour the chicken juices over the rice. Using the handle of a wooden spoon, poke a few holes in the pyramid of rice reaching to the bottom of the pot. Cover and increase the heat to medium-high. Cook covered for 10 minutes, watching closely, as tahdig can burn very quickly. Reduce the heat to medium, cover the bottom of the lid with a clean kitchen towel and place firmly back on the pot. Continue to cook for 10 minutes. Reduce the heat to low and cook for 40 minutes.

Scatter the rice mixture on a serving platter. Gently scoop out the tahdig, arrange on the side, and serve.

# NARGESI (SPINACH NARCISSUS)

**SERVES 4**

## METHOD

Heat the oil in a large pan over medium-high heat. Add the onion and sauté, stirring often, for 10 minutes or until browned. Reduce the heat to medium-low, add the garlic, and sauté, stirring constantly and reducing the heat as needed, for 3 minutes or until golden. Increase the heat to medium, add the butter and melt. Add the spinach in batches, covering the pan for about 30 seconds after adding each batch to allow it to wilt. Add the turmeric, nutmeg, lemon juice, ½ teaspoon salt, and ¼ teaspoon pepper and stir to combine. Cook, uncovered, for 3 to 5 minutes or until most of the liquid has evaporated. If the spinach releases a lot of liquid, increase the heat to medium-high to cook it off.

Using a spatula or wooden spoon, create 4 small spaces in the spinach mixture then crack an egg into each space. Season to taste with salt and pepper, cover, and cook over medium heat for 6 to 8 minutes or until the whites have set and the yolks are runny.

Remove the pan from the heat. Add a few dollops of Greek yogurt, sprinkle with sumac, garnish with dried rose petals, if using, and serve.

## INGREDIENTS

3 tablespoons olive oil

1 medium onion, sliced

1 large clove garlic, thinly sliced

1 tablespoon unsalted butter

1½ pounds (680 g) baby spinach

¼ teaspoon ground turmeric

⅛ teaspoon ground nutmeg

1½ teaspoons freshly squeezed lemon juice

Fine sea salt

Ground pepper

4 large eggs

Greek yogurt, for topping

Ground sumac, for garnish

Dried rose petals, for garnish (optional)

*Narges is the Persian word for the narcissus flower. This humble dish of spinach and eggs captures the Iranian love for beautiful, lush, fragrant gardens. The bright yellow yolk and the whites of the eggs paint a picture of a springtime narcissus, resting in a field of greens, which are represented by the spinach. Enjoy this with a side of barbari bread (a type of Persian flatbread) for brunch, or with a side of basmati rice for a light dinner.*

Marcella Lee lives in Richmond, Virginia, but her blog is as much a travelogue as it is a lexicon of international recipes and flavors. She's inspired by the places she visits, and her deft adaptation of cookbook and other found recipes demonstrates a confidence in the kitchen that encourages readers to don their aprons. This is not to say Lee's blog isn't also just fun to read. She's a natural at food blogging, combining off-the-cuff introductions with detailed recipe notes, precise instructions, and options for tweaking flavors or ingredients. Along the way, Lee revisits her Korean heritage, and notes that the foods kids used to make fun of her for eating at the lunch table—the *nori* her mother would pack in her lunch bag instead of Fritos—are precisely the flavors food lovers from Virginia to Vancouver are obsessed with today. Lee has an intrinsic sense for how to use flavors that American palates once disdained, such as fish sauce or fermented tofu. She's also unafraid of experimentation. Recently, she found a teal-colored emu egg at her local Vietnamese market and brought it home. The layered and rolled omelet she made with its contents was described as extremely eggy and light, but not something she'd ever make again. This is what food blogging should be like: uninhibited and open, with a broad appetite for both food and culture. *Broad Appetite* is a 2014 winner of the *Saveur* Best Food Blogs Best New Blog.

# Broad Appetite

Marcella Lee
Richmond, Virginia, United States
www.broadappetite.com

---

## Q+A

**What is the most treasured item in your kitchen?**
My cast iron pots and pans. It's the only piece of kitchenware I would pass on to my children.

**What is your ultimate comfort food?**
Hands down—ramen! It doesn't matter if it's the instant variety or served by a Japanese noodle master; it always sets my mood straight.

**Name a utensil you can't live without.**
Chopsticks. I use them to scramble eggs, turn over meat, and plate with precision.

**What is your go-to cocktail?**
When it comes to cocktails, I gravitate toward "old man" drinks: Moscow mules, salty dogs, and old fashioneds. What that says about me, I don't know . . .

**Who is your culinary idol?**
My culinary idol is Andy Ricker, chef and owner of Pok Pok in Portland, Oregon. He's a white guy who cooks like a Thai grandmother and is proud of it. That's something I can respect!

# BROAD APPETITE

SERVES 2

## INGREDIENTS

*For the waffles*

2 cups (260 g) all-purpose flour

4 teaspoons baking powder

¼ teaspoon salt

1¾ cups (415 ml) whole milk

½ cup (115 g) unsalted butter, melted

2 large eggs

2 tablespoons granulated sugar

1 teaspoon vanilla extract

*For the fried chicken*

2 to 4 cups (½ to 1 L) vegetable oil, for frying

2 cloves garlic, finely chopped

1-inch (2.5 cm) piece fresh ginger, finely grated

3 tablespoons soy sauce

3 tablespoons gochujang (Korean chile bean paste)

3 tablespoons honey

1½ tablespoons rice wine vinegar

1 tablespoon sesame oil

1 tablespoon white sesame seeds

4 skinless, boneless chicken thighs

⅔ cup (160 ml) water

⅔ cup (85 g) all-purpose flour

2 tablespoons cornstarch

2 large eggs

# KOREAN FRIED CHICKEN AND WAFFLE SANDWICHES WITH FRIED EGGS

## METHOD

Preheat a waffle iron.

For the waffles, in a large bowl, whisk together the flour, baking powder, and salt. In a medium bowl, whisk together the milk, butter, eggs, sugar, and vanilla. Add to the flour mixture and whisk just until a batter forms.

Spray the preheated waffle iron with cooking spray. Pour ¼ of the batter into the iron and cook for 5 to 7 minutes or until golden brown. Repeat with the remaining batter to make 3 more waffles.

For the fried chicken, heat 1 inch vegetable oil in a large, heavy-bottom sauté pan over medium-high heat.

For the gochujang sauce, in a small bowl, whisk together the garlic, ginger, soy sauce, gochujang, honey, rice wine vinegar, sesame oil, and sesame seeds until smooth. Set aside.

Pound each chicken thigh to an even ¾-inch (2 cm) thickness. In a medium bowl, whisk together the water, flour, and cornstarch to create a thin paste. Dip the chicken thighs into the flour mixture, shaking off any excess. When the oil is hot, working in batches so as not to overcrowd the pan, carefully place the chicken in the oil and fry for 6 minutes or until golden brown. Transfer to paper towels to drain. Bring the oil back up to temperature and, in batches, re-fry the chicken for an additional 6 minutes or until golden brown. Transfer to paper towels to drain.

*If you've never had Korean fried chicken, you're in for a treat. It's double fried with a cornstarch batter that gives it an exceptional crunch. The crust holds up beautifully to the sweet and spicy sauce and the waffle "bun" makes the whole mess easy to eat. I'm thrilled with the results and think the sandwich is a fitting fusion of my Korean and Southern roots.*

For the fried eggs, spray a nonstick skillet with cooking spray and place over medium heat. Add the eggs to the pan, reduce the heat to low, and cook for a few minutes or until the whites are starting to set. Flip the eggs and cook until the whites are firm and opaque but the yolk is still runny, about 30 seconds. Remove from the heat.

Place the fried chicken in a medium bowl, add the gochujang sauce, and toss to coat—mind that the chicken is completely coated in sauce. Place 2 pieces of chicken on each waffle and top each with a fried egg. Pour any excess sauce over the chicken and eggs then top with the remaining waffles and serve immediately.

# SESAME AND CHIA TOFFEE

SERVES 10

## METHOD

Line a baking sheet with parchment paper or foil and lightly butter the parchment or foil. Arrange the tea biscuits, side by side, on the baking sheet and set aside.

In a medium saucepan, combine the sugar, butter, and corn syrup and place over medium heat. Cook, stirring occasionally, until the mixture is a rich golden color and a candy thermometer registers 305°F (150°C). Immediately pour the toffee over the biscuits and spread evenly with a spatula. When the toffee is comfortable to the touch but still soft, sprinkle with sesame and chia seeds, gently pressing the seeds into the toffee with your fingers.

Place the toffee in the refrigerator and chill until firm. Break into rustic, uneven pieces and enjoy. This can be made 1 to 3 days in advance and should be stored in an airtight container in a cool area.

## INGREDIENTS

20 tea biscuits

¾ cup (150 g) granulated sugar

½ cup (115 g) unsalted butter, cut into small pieces

1 tablespoon dark corn syrup

¼ cup (65 g) sesame seeds, preferably a combination of white and black

2 tablespoons (30 g) chia seeds

*They say you're either a cook or a baker and I definitely fall on the "cook" end of the spectrum. I love making this toffee because it's a cook's dessert. You make the toffee on the stovetop, pour it over cookies, and top with what- ever strikes your fancy. The sesame and chia seeds give this dish a unique nutty flavor and make for a distinctive presentation, especially if you use a combination of white and black sesame seeds.*

CANNELLE
ET VANILLE

# Cannelle et Vanille

Aran Goyoaga
Seattle, Washington, United States
www.cannellevanille.com

In 1998 Aran Goyoaga moved to the United States from the Basque region of Spain and not long after started a blog to catalog her aesthetic sensibilities, flavor inspirations, and original recipes. Gift guides, foraging guides, dining recommendations, travelogues, and kid-friendly options— approved by Goyoaga's two children—are also regular features of *Cannelle et Vanille* (French for cinnamon and vanilla, the smells she associates with her grandparents' pastry shop in the Basque Country). The photography is and has always been incredibly vivid. Goyoaga really knows how to capture the slippery swirls of long pasta swimming in sauce, the craggy flakes of a crostata crust, the crumbs on a forkful of crumb cake, and the crisp edges of freshly cut vegetables, so it makes sense that she teaches photography and food styling workshops on the side. An omnivore who dabbles in gluten- and dairy-free meals, Goyoaga tends to feature vegetable- and fruit-forward recipes like Roasted Broccoli Rabe Tostada with Avocado, Fried Egg, and Chimichurri; Citrus Cake for the Winter Blues (sprinkled with rose petals!); and Fiddlehead Ferns, Nettles, and Ricotta Gnudi. Inspiration on how to set a table, arrange a bouquet, or picnic al fresco abounds. *Cannelle et Vanille* is the kind of blog you want to dive into on a lazy Sunday morning and be cooking from later that day. Goyoaga is the author of *Small Plates and Sweet Treats*, which was published in 2012. *Cannelle et Vanille* has been a James Beard Award finalist, and been featured on Martha Stewart's *Everyday Food*, *Good Morning America*, and in the *New York Times*.

## Q+A

**What is the most treasured item in your kitchen?**
My knives and my KitchenAid mixer. I keep my knives really sharp and my mixer sparkly clean. It comes from all the years in the professional pastry kitchen.

**What is your ultimate comfort food?**
Definitely a super-hot bowl of pho in the cold months.

**What is your go-to cocktail?**
I am much more of a wine or cider person, but if I have to pick a cocktail, I'd say Paloma.

**Name a utensil you can't live without.**
Probably a mandoline. Or wait, maybe even a special tasting spoon I have had for years.

**What is your go-to breakfast?**
Eggs! Fried eggs are my favorite with a little bit of chili oil and dukkah spice.

**Who is your culinary idol?**
Right now I love what Renee Erickson, Rachel Yang, and Matt Dillon are doing in Seattle. Lee Desrosiers and Camille Becerra in NYC. And Sébastien Canonne of the French Pastry School in Chicago.

# PEAR AND HAZELNUT FRANGIPANE TART

SERVES 8

## INGREDIENTS

*For the gluten-free dough*

1 cup (140 g) superfine brown rice flour

2 tablespoons potato starch

2 tablespoons tapioca starch

1 tablespoon granulated sugar

½ teaspoon salt

½ cup (115 g) unsalted butter, cold and cut into small pieces

3 to 4 tablespoons (45 to 60 ml) ice-cold water

*For the filling*

1 cup (110 g) ground hazelnuts, plus 7 tablespoons (60 g) roughly chopped, toasted hazelnuts

½ cup (115 g) unsalted butter, melted and cooled

½ cup (100 g) granulated sugar

1 large egg

1 tablespoon tapioca starch

Pinch of salt

3 medium pears, peeled, halved, cored, and thinly sliced crosswise

Confectioners' sugar

## METHOD

For the gluten-free tart dough, in a food processor, pulse together the brown rice flour, potato starch, tapioca starch, sugar, and salt. Add the butter and pulse about 10 times until the butter is cut into the flour mixture. Gradually add the ice water by tablespoonfuls while pulsing— mind that you may not need all of it—and continue to pulse just until the dough comes together. It should stick together when pressed, but not be too wet. Form the dough into a disk, wrap it in plastic wrap, and flatten it a bit with your hands. Refrigerate for about 1 hour.

On a lightly floured table or countertop, use a rolling pin to roll out the dough into a ⅛ to ¼-inch-thick (3 to 6 mm) round, large enough to line a 9-inch (22.5 cm) tart pan, preferably with a removable bottom. Fit the dough into the tart pan, pushing it into the pan, especially along the edges. Don't worry if the dough cracks; just pinch it back together. Refrigerate the tart shell for 20 minutes while you make the filling.

Set a rack in the middle of the oven and preheat the oven to 375°F (190°C).

For the pear and hazelnut frangipane filling, in a food processor, combine the ground hazelnuts, butter, sugar, egg, tapioca starch, and salt and pulse until smooth. Spread the frangipane filling inside the chilled tart shell. Arrange the pear slices in clusters on top of the frangipane filling, splaying the slices out slightly and lightly pressing down.

Place the tart on a baking sheet and bake on the middle rack for 40 to 45 minutes or until the top is golden brown.

Let the tart cool slightly. Sprinkle the outer edge with the chopped hazelnuts, dust with powdered sugar, and serve.

*Hazelnut and pear make for a dreamy combination, but you can use different kinds of fruit, including berries, apples, most stone fruit, and even poached quince. You can swap in almonds or pistachios in place of the hazelnut.*

SERVES
4 TO 6

# NEW RECIPE
# RICOTTA GNUDI WITH FAVA BEANS AND PEAS

## INGREDIENTS

*For the ricotta gnudi*

1 pound (450 g) ricotta

1 ounce (30 g) freshly grated Parmesan

1 large egg

1 large egg yolk

¾ teaspoon salt

½ teaspoon ground pepper

7 tablespoons (70 g) potato starch

*For the favas and peas*

1 cup shelled fresh fava beans (1 pound / 450 g in the pod)

1 cup shelled fresh peas (1 pound / 450 g in the pod)

1 tablespoon unsalted butter

2 tablespoons olive oil

3 cloves garlic or 1 head spring garlic, thinly sliced

Salt

Ground pepper

2 tablespoons finely chopped flat-leaf parsley leaves

1 tablespoon finely chopped chives

1 ounce (30 g) freshly grated Parmesan

## METHOD

For the ricotta gnudi, combine the ricotta, Parmesan, egg, egg yolk, salt, and pepper in a medium bowl and whisk to combine. Add the potato starch and stir with a spoon until incorporated. The dough should be moist and loose.

Line a baking sheet with parchment paper and dust with potato starch. Take a tablespoon of the dough and using two soup spoons, shape it into a little dumpling that resembles a quenelle—they don't need to be perfect. Place the gnudi on the parchment-lined baking sheet and continue to make gnudi with the rest of the dough—you should have about 30 gnudi. Cover the gnudi loosely with plastic wrap.

For the fava beans and peas, bring a large pot of water to a boil and prepare a bowl of ice water. When the water comes to a boil, add a large pinch of salt then add the fava beans and cook for 2 to 4 minutes, depending on the size, or until tender. Use a slotted spoon to scoop the fava beans from the boiling water and immediately plunge them into the ice water to stop the cooking process. Reserve the boiling water and add more ice to the ice water.

Add the peas to the boiling water and cook for 2 minutes or until tender. Use a slotted spoon to scoop the peas from the boiling water and immediately plunge them into the ice water to stop the cooking process. Reserve the boiling water. Drain the peas and favas. Peel and discard the outer skins of the fava beans and place both the fava beans and the peas in a bowl.

Working in batches if necessary, cook the gnudi in the boiling water until they rise to the surface of the water, about 3 to 4 minutes. Continue cooking for another 2 minutes, and then use a slotted spoon to scoop the gnudi from the boiling water onto a clean plate. Reserve the boiling water and repeat with the remaining gnudi.

In a large sauté pan, heat the butter and olive oil over medium-high heat. Add the garlic and sauté for 1 minute or until translucent. Add the fava beans and peas and cook for 1 more minute. Season to taste with salt and pepper then add the parsley, chives, and gnudi, stir, and cook for 1 more minute. Sprinkle with the Parmesan and serve immediately.

These pillowy gnudi are one of the easiest things you can make for a dinner party, plus it's fun to get the children involved. They're so versatile you can pair them with any vegetable or simple sauce—browned butter and fresh sage make a particularly perfect match. As written, this recipe is gluten-free, but if you can eat wheat, use an equal amount of all-purpose flour in place of the potato starch.

A self-described New Orleans-born, part-Cajun girl living in Portland, Oregon, Brooke Bass brings a farm-to-table sensibility to her site, which features art-quality photographs as well as tasteful stories about her friends, family, and the gatherings they share. As the name might suggest, Bass isn't afraid of unique flavor pairings: Black Garlic Ice Cream with Oreo Cookie Crumble, Fried Catfish in Lettuce Cups with Sauce Gribiche, Cabernet-Braised Short Rib and Chanterelle Cobbler, and Chicory- and Cocoa-rubbed Wagyu Fillet are all recent features which blend an outside-the-box thought process with recipes that work. Beside these inspired experiments are more traditional recipes for the Best Damn Buttermilk Biscuits, Garlic White Pizza with Chanterelles and Arugula, Moroccan Moules Frites with Sherry, and a gorgeous Strawberry Jam Tart with Cornmeal Crust and Vanilla Ricotta Cream. One category that stands out in Bass's repertoire are comfort foods in bowls. An unofficial category, it's the kind of food you want to get cozy with on your couch on a chilly night: Uni Grits with Crispy Prosciutto and Bonito Broth, Lamb and Sausage Gumbo, Tom Kha Gai (Thai Coconut Chicken Soup), and Seafood Fricot with Summer Sea Beans, a French chowder-like soup. Between recipe posts are travel guides and tales of some of Bass's dining adventures. Unexpected but delicious to look at, *Chocolate + Marrow* has been a finalist in *Saveur*'s Best Food Blog Awards and has been featured in Life & Thyme, Food | Yahoo Style, and Food52.

# Chocolate + Marrow

Brooke Bass
Portland, Oregon, United States
www.chocolateandmarrow.com

===== Q+A =====

### What is the most treasured item in your kitchen?
An Eskimo-style knife that I purchased in Alaska with carbon steel and one of the most beautiful handles I've ever seen.

### Name a utensil you can't live without.
I have this very tiny whisk that my hair stylist gave me. He gets them for free to blend color and saw me eyeing it one day. It's not anything expensive or fancy but it's probably the most handy thing I have in my whole kitchen and I use it nearly every day (it's the absolute best for salad dressings!).

### What is your ultimate comfort food?
I am a comfort food junkie, so this is hard to choose, but I think my go-to would have to be *really* buttery high-quality grits with fried lardons.

### What is your go-to cocktail?
Vodka martini with olives. Just don't let me have more than two. (Or do?)

### Who is your culinary icon?
I think I'd have to go with Julia Child. I just love the fortitude and persistence with which she approached food and cooking and finding her place in an industry that wasn't always welcoming to her.

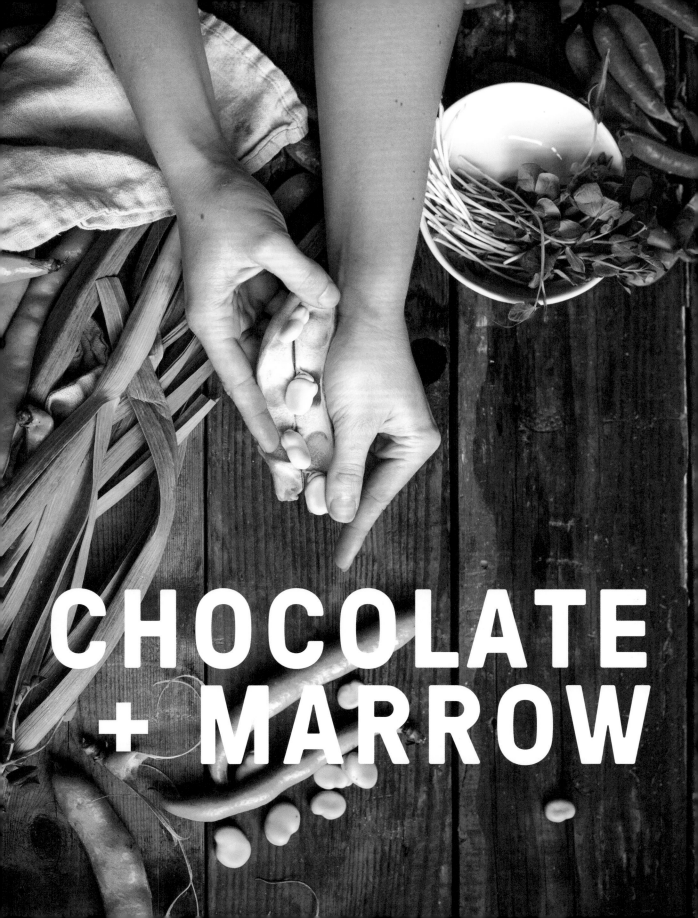

# CHOCOLATE
# + MARROW

# FRIED OYSTER BRIOCHE TOAST WITH FENNEL-TOMATO SALAD

**MAKES 6 TOASTS**

## METHOD

Remove fava beans from their pods. Add beans to a pot of boiling water and boil 2 to 3 minutes, or until the outer skin appears slightly wrinkled. Peel skin from the fava bean and transfer to a medium bowl with tomatoes, fennel, olive oil, and lemon juice. Season the salad with salt and pepper and gently toss to combine.

For the oysters, fill a Dutch oven or deep fryer with 1½ inches (4 cm) canola oil and place over medium-high heat until oil reaches approximately 350°F.

In a small bowl, whisk together the cornmeal, flour, salt, pepper, garlic powder, and cayenne pepper.

When the oil is hot, working in batches, toss the oysters in the flour mixture then fry for about 2 minutes or until golden brown. Transfer to paper towels to drain. Repeat with the remaining oysters.

For the toast, melt the butter in a large skillet over medium heat. Working in batches, toast the brioche, flipping it often and adding more butter as necessary, for 3 to 4 minutes or until golden.

Spread a smear of mayonnaise on each slice of toast then top with the salad and 2 to 3 fried oysters. Garnish with the chopped fennel fronds and serve with hot sauce on the side.

*I grew up in New Orleans, a city that has a deep history with oysters. In fact, one of my earliest memories of eating oysters comes from my second-grade science class, in which part of the lesson was to scoop the cold briny flesh from its shell, lay it atop a saltine cracker, and splash a few hits of hot sauce on top.*

*As an adult I can't fully understand what was particularly "science-y" about this, but it didn't matter back then. It was love at first bite. For this updated and decidedly more grown-up version, the fried oyster rests on a slice of buttery brioche and is finished with a bright, fresh salad of fennel, fava beans, and tomato. It makes me realize just how special these little bivalves truly are. I've also been known to make just the salad and fried oysters, skipping the bread, which is good for days when you want to eat "light."*

## INGREDIENTS

*For the salad*

1 pound (450 g) fresh fava beans in the pod

1 cup (180 grams) cherry tomatoes, halved

½ fennel bulb, cored and thinly sliced, fronds reserved and finely chopped for garnish

1 tablespoon olive oil

1 tablespoon freshly squeezed lemon juice

Kosher salt

Ground pepper

*For the oysters*

About 4½ cups (1 L) canola oil, for frying

¾ cup (130 g) yellow cornmeal

2 tablespoons all-purpose flour

1 tablespoon kosher salt or ½ teaspoon table salt

1 teaspoon ground pepper

1 teaspoon garlic powder

½ teaspoon cayenne pepper

18 small oysters (or large oysters, cut into bite-size pieces)

*For the toast*

4 tablespoons (55 g) unsalted butter, plus more as needed

6 slices brioche (½-inch / 12 mm thick)

½ cup (110 g) mayonnaise

1 tablespoon hot sauce, such as Tabasco

## NEW RECIPE

# BLISTERED GREEN BEANS WITH BURRATA AND SHERRY-NECTARINE VINAIGRETTE

**SERVES 4**

## INGREDIENTS

*For the sherry-nectarine vinaigrette*

About 1 cup (240 ml) extra-dry sherry

1 nectarine, cut into chunks

1 tablespoon apple cider vinegar

½ jalapeño, seeds removed and roughly chopped

Salt

Ground pepper

⅓ cup (75 ml) olive oil

*For the green beans*

1 tablespoon olive or canola oil

1 pound (450 g) fresh green beans, trimmed

Salt

4 ounces (110 g) Burrata or other soft fresh mild cheese, such as goat or mozzarella

1 nectarine, cut into wedges

1½ jalapeños, cut into paper-thin rounds

¼ cup (30 g) almonds, preferably Marcona, crushed

Minced chives (optional)

## METHOD

For the vinaigrette, in a small bowl or airtight container, pour enough sherry over the nectarine chunks to completely cover the fruit. Cover and let sit until softened, about 2 hours at room temperature or overnight in the refrigerator. Drain the nectarines and transfer to a blender; discard the sherry. Add the vinegar and jalapeño to the blender and purée until a smooth paste forms. Season to taste with salt and pepper then transfer to a small bowl and slowly whisk in the olive oil, a few drops at a time, until fully incorporated.

For the green beans, heat the oil in a large sauté pan over medium-high heat. Add the green beans and cook, undisturbed, for 6 minutes or until beginning to blister and char. Stir, then continue cooking for another 6 minutes or until tender. Season liberally with salt. Transfer to a platter and top with the Burrata, nectarine wedges, jalapeño rounds and seeds, and almonds. Drizzle with the vinaigrette, garnish with the chives, if using, and serve.

*Sometimes I fall into a rut when cooking green beans. I'll pull them from the trellis that sits outside my house, stare into the bowl, and think, "Oh I'll just toss them with some olive oil and salt and call it a day." While that's all fine and good, I've recently found myself wanting to take it up a notch, making big salads that highlight green beans, but also incorporate lots of colorful, fresh ingredients. Then during dinner at one of my favorite Portland restaurants, Grain and Gristle, I found inspiration for doing just that.*

*For this salad, I sauté the green beans to tenderize and flavor them, but you could grill them instead. The cooked beans are then topped with nectarine wedges, a round of burrata, several thin slices of jalapeño, and crunchy Marcona almonds. The whole dish is drizzled with a sweet yet smoky sherry-nectarine vinaigrette. Hot, cold, or room temperature—this is a dish that elevates green beans to a level way above simple salt and olive oil.*

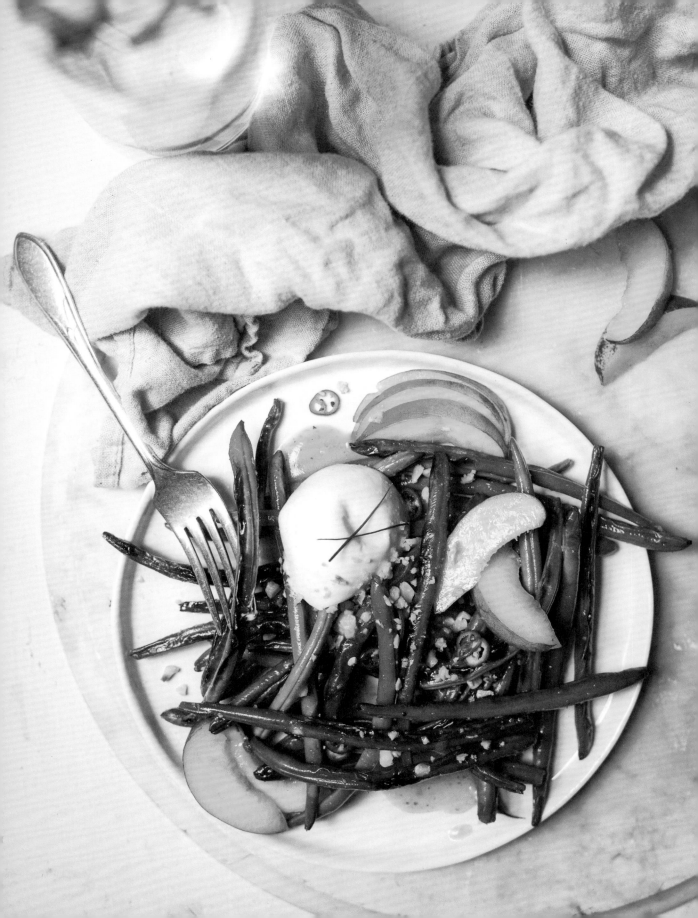

# THE
# CLEVER
# CARROT

# The Clever Carrot

**Emilie Raffa**
New York, New York, United States
www.theclevercarrot.com

Emilie Raffa, a trained chef and former private chef, has dedicated her life and blog to eating a balanced diet of home-cooked food. The married mother of two is deeply inspired by her Mediterranean background. Dishes are often accented with bright citrus, golden olive oil, and fresh herbs. Though she's based in New York, Raffa makes the most of each season's produce. Because she's been cooking professionally for a decade, Raffa shares useful tips and tricks in many of her recipes. A recipe for roasted carrots yields two meals (citrus roasted rainbow carrots and a creamy roasted carrot soup) instead of just one. More challenging recipes, such as brioche rolls, come with step-by-step instructions and exuberant encouragement. Thanks to copious testing and a hoard of fans who regularly comment, Raffa's recipes are foolproof delights. Though she features many fruit desserts on the blog, one category that's unique to *The Clever Carrot* are Raffa's recipes for breakfast cookies. Seeded, whole-grain, or granola-inspired, they're a simple breakfast solution for kids and adults alike. *The Clever Carrot* was a finalist for Best Food Photography in the annual *Saveur* Best Food Blog Awards and has been featured in *Oprah Magazine*, Food52, *Food & Wine* magazine, and many other publications. Raffa is the author of *The Clever Cookbook*, and is also a regular contributor to the digital cooking publication *feedfeed*.

---

## Q+A

**What is the most treasured item in your kitchen?**
My Dutch oven.

**What is your ultimate comfort food?**
Freshly baked sourdough bread with salted butter.

**What is your go-to breakfast?**
Mango and banana smoothie (after coffee, of course).

**Name a utensil you can't live without.**
Tongs!

**What is your go-to cocktail?**
Margarita on the rocks, no salt.

**Who would you love to cook for?**
My grandmothers.

# ITALIAN ALMOND RICOTTA CAKE, MY WAY

## INGREDIENTS

1 cup (200 g) granulated sugar, plus more for sprinkling

½ cup (115 g) unsalted butter, melted

Zest of 2 lemons, preferably organic and unwaxed

1 capful pure almond extract

Pinch of salt

4 large eggs

1 cup (245 g) ricotta

1½ cups (150 g) ground skin-on almonds

1 cup (130 g) all-purpose flour

1½ teaspoons baking powder

¼ cup (25 g) sliced almonds, plus more for sprinkling on top

Confectioners' sugar

## METHOD

Preheat the oven to 350°F (180°C). Butter the bottom and sides of a 9-inch (23 cm) springform pan and sprinkle with sugar.

In a large bowl, whisk together the sugar, melted butter, lemon zest, almond extract, and salt. Add the eggs, 1 at a time, incorporating each egg before adding the next one, and beat for 2 to 3 minutes or until creamy. Add the ricotta and whisk vigorously until there are no lumps—mind that a few small lumps are OK, but the batter shouldn't look like cottage cheese. Add the ground almonds, flour, and baking powder and stir gently to combine. Scrape the batter into the prepared pan and sprinkle with the sliced almonds. Bake for 35 to 40 minutes or until a skewer inserted in the center comes out almost clean. Let the cake cool in the pan for at least 15 minutes then take it out of the pan and let cool completely.

Dust the cake with confectioners' sugar, top with sliced almonds, cut into slices, and serve.

*This dessert is a twist on classic Italian ricotta cake, with a few shortcuts to make life easier—there are no egg whites to whip and the entire recipe is made in one bowl. The crumb is soft and velvety, while the delicate flavor is kissed with the delightful scent of almond and lemon. It's best served the same day it's made, with a side of strawberries and freshly whipped cream.*

*The recipe calls for skin-on almonds, which account for the cake's dark chestnut color. You can also use blanched almonds for a more "blonde" look. For accurate measuring, gently spoon the ground almonds into your measuring cup and avoid packing them down.*

# CHICKPEA AND ROASTED RED PEPPER SALAD

SERVES
2 TO 4

## METHOD

For the vinaigrette, whisk together the olive oil, red wine vinegar, and oregano. Season to taste with salt and pepper.

In a large bowl, toss together the chickpeas, roasted red peppers, celery, and sliced mint. Drizzle with the vinaigrette, season to taste with salt and pepper, and let marinate at room temperature for 30 minutes.

Just before serving, toast the bread until golden then drizzle with olive oil and rub with the cut side of the garlic. Slice the bread in half and arrange around the salad. Sprinkle the salad with more mint and the reserved celery leaves, season to taste with salt and pepper, and serve.

## INGREDIENTS

*For the vinaigrette*

2½ tablespoons olive oil

1 tablespoon red wine vinegar

½ teaspoon dried oregano

Coarse salt

Ground pepper

*For the salad*

14 ounces (400 g) drained and rinsed canned chickpeas

½ cup (95 g) chopped marinated roasted red peppers

1 medium rib celery, trimmed (leaves reserved) and thinly sliced

¼ cup fresh mint leaves, thinly sliced, plus more for garnish

Coarse salt

Ground pepper

2 slices sourdough bread

Olive oil, for drizzling

1 clove garlic, cut in half lengthwise

*This dish combines the many delicious tastes of the Mediterranean all in one bowl. The secret is to let the salad marinate before serving, which gives the veggies time to drink in the flavors of vibrant fresh mint and woodsy oregano. For extra flavor, use roasted red peppers that have been marinated in garlic and herbs. And don't skip the sourdough—it's perfect for mopping up any extra vinaigrette.*

As if propelled by a beauty in the world only she can glean, Meike Peters puts her food life online each week at *Eat in My Kitchen*, a beautiful blog that documents her nuanced recipes and meticulous stories. Peters lives in Berlin but summers in Malta, an archipelago in the Mediterranean. Her recipes are both breezy and precise—seasonings and accents are depicted and translated with the precision of a knowing cook, but not one without foibles. Peters's dedication to creating seasonal, inspired recipes is contagious. Few bloggers manage both to draw readers in and actually get them to cook in their kitchens, but Peters is a natural. Perhaps this is because she cooks to eat; an omnivorous appetite and memories of her mother's cooking inspire many of her recipes. Equally important is the sensuality of cooking, which comes out in recipes like Elderflower Lime Cake, a floral weekend-style pound cake tenderized with buttermilk and brightened with lime juice. In her Bacon, Egg, and Cheese Sandwich with Garden Vegetables, Peters tops crusty, whole-grain bread rolls with slices of pungent cheese, eggs fried until lacy around the edges, thinly shaved cucumbers, avocado, and crisp bacon. The eggs are peppered, the bread is drizzled with olive oil and soaks up the drippings from the bacon. It's just the thing you want to eat after a long work week. When she's in Malta, Peters adopts a thoroughly Mediterranean lifestyle. A recipe for Grouper with Watermelon, Basil, and Mint captures the island life better than any beach vacation. With regular updates and exuberant prose Peters is a great near-daily read. Peters's first book, *Eat in My Kitchen: To Cook, to Bake, to Eat, and to Treat* was released in the fall of 2016.

# Eat In My Kitchen

Meike Peters
Berlin, Germany
www.eatinmykitchen.meikepeters.com

---

### Q+A

**What is your ultimate comfort food?**
Pizza—made from scratch, every Sunday evening.

**Name a utensil you can't live without.**
My large wooden chopping block and a long sharp knife.

**What is your go-to breakfast?**
Green tea with freshly squeezed lemon.

**What is your go-to cocktail?**
Champagne with puréed fresh strawberries.

**Who is your culinary idol?**
My mother.

# EAT
# IN MY
# KITCHEN

SERVES
2 TO 4

## INGREDIENTS

*For the filling*

1¼ pounds (570 g) peeled and seeded butternut squash, or Hokkaido with skin, cut into ½-inch (12 mm) cubes

Olive oil

Flaky sea salt

2 tablespoons unsalted butter

30 large fresh sage leaves

4 heaping tablespoons fresh ricotta

3 ounces (85 g) freshly grated Parmesan

A few black peppercorns, crushed with a mortar and pestle

*For the béchamel sauce*

2½ cups (600 ml) whole milk

Pinch of nutmeg, preferably freshly grated, plus more to taste

Fine sea salt

Ground pepper

2 tablespoons unsalted butter

¼ cup (30 g) all-purpose flour

1 large bay leaf

*For the crespelle*

⅔ cup (160 ml) whole milk

2 large eggs

1 cup (130 g) all-purpose flour, sifted

¼ teaspoon fine sea salt

Unsalted butter, to cook the crespelle

# PUMPKIN RICOTTA CRESPELLE WITH CRISPY SAGE

## METHOD

Preheat the oven to 400°F (200°C). Line a baking sheet with parchment paper.

For the filling, place the squash on the lined baking sheet and toss with 2 tablespoons olive oil. Season to taste with flaky sea salt and roast for about 25 minutes or until soft. Set the squash aside; keep the oven set to 400°F (200°C).

For the béchamel sauce, combine the milk, nutmeg, and pinches of salt and pepper in a medium saucepan and bring to a boil. Immediately take the pan off the heat and set aside.

To make the roux for the béchamel, melt the butter in a separate medium saucepan over medium-high heat and as soon as it's sizzling hot, whisk in the flour. Slowly pour the hot milk mixture into the roux and whisk until smooth. Add the bay leaf and simmer on low, whisking occasionally, for 2 to 3 minutes or until the sauce starts to thicken. Remove and discard the bay leaf. Season to taste with additional nutmeg, salt, and pepper then cover and set aside.

For the crespelle, whisk together the milk and eggs in a large bowl. Add the flour and salt and beat with an electric mixer until smooth. Let the batter sit for about 10 minutes before you cook the crespelle.

To cook the crespelle, melt ½ teaspoon butter in a large cast iron or nonstick pan over medium-high heat. Pour in a ladle of the batter, tilting and turning the pan, so that the batter spreads evenly and very thinly. Cook the crespelle for 30 to 60 seconds per side or until golden then transfer to a plate. Finish making 3 more crespelle, adjusting the heat as necessary and adding a little more butter to the pan between crespelle.

*Filled Italian crespelle are a rich pleasure. You can eat them all year round and fill them with almost any produce that nature offers, but to me, this comfort food is right for autumn and winter. So the vegetables of the cold season, like squash, spinach, or mushrooms, are more likely to find their way into my pancake rolls.*

To assemble the crespelle, in a small saucepan, heat the 2 tablespoons butter over high heat until sizzling. Add the sage leaves and fry for a few seconds or until crisp and golden but not dark. Transfer the sage to a plate.

Butter a baking dish that's large enough to fit 4 rolled crespelle. One after the other, lay each crespelle flat on a large plate, spread with ¼ of the roasted squash and drizzle with 2½ tablespoons of the béchamel sauce. Sprinkle with ¼ of the ricotta, 4 sage leaves, and a bit less than ¼ of the Parmesan. Season to taste with crushed peppercorns. Roll into tight wraps and place next to each other in the buttered baking dish. Pour the remaining béchamel sauce over the crespelle and sprinkle with the remaining Parmesan. Bake for 12 minutes. Turn on the broiler for the last 1 to 2 minutes to brown and crisp the top. Sprinkle with the remaining sage and serve.

# PEAR-STAR ANISE BREAKFAST CAKE

SERVES 6 TO 8

## METHOD

Preheat the oven to 350°F (180°C), preferably on convection setting. Butter an 8-inch (20 cm) springform pan.

For the topping, in a small bowl, whisk together the 2 tablespoons sugar, half the star anise, and ½ teaspoon of the cinnamon; set aside.

In a medium bowl, whisk together the remaining star anise and cinnamon, along with the flour, cornstarch, baking powder, and sea salt.

In a large bowl, use an electric mixer to beat the butter and the remaining ½ cup sugar until fluffy. Add the eggs, 1 at a time, incorporating each egg before adding the next one, and continue beating for a few minutes or until thick, creamy, and light yellow. Add the flour mixture and continue mixing for 2 minutes or until the batter is well combined then scrape the batter into the buttered pan.

Use a thin, sharp knife to score the outside of each pear half lengthwise 4 times. Arrange the pear halves, scored-side up, in a circle on top of the cake. Sprinkle with the reserved star anise-cinnamon sugar topping and bake for about 40 minutes (slightly longer if using a conventional oven) or until golden on top. If you insert a skewer in the center of the cake, it should come out clean. Let the cake cool for a few minutes before taking it out of the pan.

Enjoy the cake on its own, or topped with sweetened whipped cream or vanilla ice cream.

## INGREDIENTS

½ cup (100 g) granulated sugar, plus 2 tablespoons for the topping

1 teaspoon finely ground star anise, about 5 pods ground with a mortar and pestle

1 teaspoon ground cinnamon

1 cup (130 g) all-purpose flour

¼ cup (30 g) cornstarch

1 heaping teaspoon baking powder

⅛ teaspoon fine sea salt

⅔ cup (160 g) unsalted butter, at room temperature

3 large eggs

2 firm pears, peeled, cored, and cut in half lengthwise

*This cake is practically made for a cozy Sunday breakfast. The addition of cornstarch keeps it light, while the combination of pears, cinnamon, and star anise adds fragrant fruitiness. Feel free to follow the seasons, and replace the pears with apples, plums, or peaches. In the spring, you could use strawberries or blueberries, however, I would skip the wintery star anise in that case and only use cinnamon. The baking time might need a little adjustment, but as long as you check the cake with a skewer before you pull it out of the oven, you should be safe.*

*Fruit cakes have a long tradition in Germany. Often baked on a tray, they typically feature a layer of sweet yeast dough topped with juicy fruit that softens in the oven. It makes for a nice summer treat, but I prefer using sponge cake for the base. It's light and airy, plus it offers the right balance of cake to fruit and just enough sweetness, especially when it's covered in a thin spiced-sugar crust.*

Phoebe Lapine is a self-described competitive french fry eater who also develops recipes for magazines and runs a catering business out of her apartment in Manhattan. Oh, and she teaches cooking classes, too. That's the sort of driven, fun-loving, carefree lust for life that Lapine brings to *Feed Me Phoebe*, a blog bursting with recipes, guides, product reviews, and diary-like entries that invites readers to follow along or simply find a healthful, gluten-free recipe to make for dinner, a date, or dessert. Guides to other cities (Los Angeles and San Juan Del Sur, Nicaragua) pop up every few months as well. Youthful readers are easily drawn into Lapine's world, where homemade Pumpkin Chai Tea Lattes flow freely and holiday recipes (Green Eggs, No Ham for St. Patrick's Day, for instance) mark each season. Lapine has a penchant for the culture of wellness, and she sets monthly goals for herself (get eight hours of sleep every night, or meditate every morning) which she tracks on the blog, being sure to detail the physical and mental results. It's clearly an inspiration to her followers, who comment and share their own journeys. *Feed Me Phoebe* has been featured in *Food & Wine* magazine, *Self*, *Cosmopolitan*, and many other publications. Lapine is the author of *In the Small Kitchen*, a recipe book, and *The Wellness Project*, a memoir.

# Feed Me Phoebe

**Phoebe Lapine**
New York, New York, United States
www.feedmephoebe.com

---

## Q+A

**What is your ultimate comfort food?**
French fries with a side of aioli.

**What is your go-to breakfast?**
I like to switch it up between full-fat Greek yogurt with homemade granola, a green smoothie, avocado toast, or a plate of leftovers with an egg on top.

**What is the most treasured item in your kitchen?**
My neurotically well-seasoned cast iron skillet.

**What is your go-to cocktail?**
A BLT. Bourbon, lemon juice, and a splash of tonic.

**Who would you love to cook for?**
Rafael Nadal. So long as his mouth is full, it won't matter if we have nothing to say to each other.

**Who is your culinary idol?**
The queen: Ina Garten.

# FEED ME
# PHOEBE

# SALMON POKE BOWLS WITH PICKLED RADISHES, AVOCADO, AND SPICY PONZU

SERVES
4

## METHOD

In a fine-mesh sieve, rinse the sushi rice under warm water until the water runs clear. Transfer to a medium saucepan, add the water, and soak for 15 minutes. Bring to a boil then reduce the heat to low, cover, and cook for 20 minutes. Remove from the heat and rest, covered, for 10 minutes then fluff with a fork and divide between 4 bowls.

While the rice is cooking, combine the carrots, radishes, garlic, vinegar, and salt in a medium bowl. Let sit, stirring occasionally, for 15 minutes or until the vegetables have softened.

For the sauce, in a medium bowl, whisk together the serrano chile peppers, tamari or soy sauce, lemon juice, and water. Transfer half the sauce to a small serving bowl. Add the salmon and cilantro to the remaining sauce and toss gently to coat.

Divide the salmon mixture, pickled vegetables, and avocado among the bowls, arranging each in its own quadrant over the rice. Spoon the reserved ponzu sauce over the poke bowls (or serve on the side), and garnish with black sesame gomashio, if using.

*My health and food philosophy comes down to eating a lot of good with just a little bad. It's a sweet spot I like to call healthy hedonism, and one that's perfectly embodied by this poke bowl. The white sushi rice is balanced out by a robust helping of colorful pickled veggies, plus two great sources of healthy fats, raw salmon and sliced avocado. The spicy ponzu, kicked up with serrano chile peppers, gives these Hawaiian-inspired bowls brightness and zip.*

*This recipe is perfect for a quick weeknight dinner, as there's not a whole lot of cooking involved. But my favorite way to serve it is on one giant platter, with toppings piled high, so guests can pick and choose their own poke bowl adventure.*

## INGREDIENTS

1 cup (200 g) sushi rice

1½ cups (355 ml) water

½ pound (225 g) peeled carrots (3 medium), diced

5 medium radishes, diced

1 clove garlic, finely chopped

3 tablespoons rice wine vinegar

1 teaspoon fine sea salt

1 pound (450 g) sashimi-grade salmon, preferably wild or organic, cut into ½-inch (1.25 cm) cubes

4 tablespoons chopped cilantro leaves

1 avocado, halved, pitted, and thinly sliced

Black sesame gomashio* (optional)

*Gomashio is a condiment of ground black sesame seeds and sea salt that can generally be found in organic food stores.

*For the sauce*

1 or 2 serrano chile peppers, thinly sliced

½ cup (120 ml) gluten-free tamari or soy sauce

½ cup (120 ml) freshly squeezed lemon juice

4 tablespoons water

# ROASTED CARROT AND FENNEL SOUP WITH FENNEL FROND GREMOLATA

**SERVES 4**

## INGREDIENTS

1 (1 pound / 450 g) fennel bulb, thinly sliced (trim and reserve the fronds)

1 pound (450 g) peeled carrots (about 6 medium), cut into 1-inch (2.5 cm) pieces

1 medium Spanish onion, thinly sliced

4 tablespoons olive oil

Fine sea salt

2 tablespoons finely chopped flat-leaf parsley leaves

1 clove garlic, finely chopped

1 tablespoon freshly grated lemon zest

3 tablespoons freshly squeezed lemon juice

Dash of cayenne

1 (½ pound / 225 g) Yukon gold potato, peeled and cut into 1-inch (2.5 cm) pieces

1 quart (950 ml) vegetable stock

3 cups (700 ml) water, plus more as needed

½ cup (120 ml) dry white wine

Sunflower seeds (optional)

## METHOD

Preheat the oven to 425°F (220°C). Line 2 baking sheets with parchment paper.

In a large mixing bowl, toss the fennel, carrots, and onion with 2 tablespoons of the olive oil and 1 teaspoon salt. Divide between the lined baking sheets and spread evenly. Roast, switching the pans from the top rack to the bottom and vice versa about halfway through cooking, for 30 to 40 minutes or until caramelized.

While the vegetables are roasting, to make the gremolata, finely chop enough of the reserved fennel fronds to measure 1 tablespoon and place in a small bowl (reserve the remaining fronds for another use or discard). Add the parsley, garlic, lemon zest and juice, the remaining 2 tablespoons olive oil, ½ teaspoon salt, and the cayenne and stir to combine.

*Back in the day, before I was diagnosed with an autoimmune disease and had to start tailoring my day job to more health-focused recipes, creamy soups were one of my favorite food groups. In winter, a velvety butternut squash and apple combination was the apple of my eye. Come summertime, I'd crush corn and clam chowder like it was my job, which it kind of was. Now that I no longer wield heavy cream with such generosity and gusto, I add potato to soups to get that luscious texture I love so much. Here, I use this "potage" strategy to update one of my old go-to recipes: roasted carrot and fennel soup.*

*Exiling the vegetables to oven purgatory gets them especially sweet, which packs even more punch when they get blended, along with that starchy potato, into a smooth purée. Instead of wasting the leafy tops of the fennel bulbs, the fronds get used in an easy Italian-inspired garlic and herb topping, making those anise flavors do double-duty. The result is a thick, satisfying spoonful that feeds my creamy soup cravings year-round.*

In a medium, heavy pot, combine the roasted vegetables with the potato, vegetable stock, water, wine, and 1 teaspoon salt. Bring to a boil then lower the heat to medium-low, cover, and cook for about 20 minutes or until the potatoes are tender.

In a food processor or blender, or using an immersion blender, purée the soup until smooth. If it's too thick, gradually add more water to reach the desired consistency. Season to taste with salt.

Ladle the soup into bowls, top with a tablespoon of gremolata, sprinkle with the sunflower seeds, if using, and serve.

# THE
# FOOD
# GAYS

# The Food Gays

Jeremy Inglett & Adrian Harris
Vancouver, British Columbia, Canada
www.foodgays.com

In just a handful of years Jeremy Inglett and Adrian Harris have racked up a bushel full of press clips and become regular contributors to Martha Stewart's recipe archive and Web site. The pair, who met at a party where they didn't know anyone else, are food obsessives based in Vancouver and partners in business as well as in life. Their blog is recipe-based, but incorporates several key lifestyle elements, such as product picks and reviews, travel diaries, gift guides, giveaways, and event announcements. As their readership grows, so too has their use of sponsored products and posts, but the recipes keep the blog feeling authentic. Their dishes lean toward one of two extremes—healthy or indulgent. Have a Super Green Smoothie Bowl for breakfast one day, and The Dirty Breakfast Sandwich or Crispy Potatoes with Prosciutto and Basil the next. Vegetarian options put spins on classics so that a bean dip gets a fuschia makeover thanks to the addition of beets, or fettuccine Alfredo goes glam with the addition of shiitake mushrooms and edible flowers. Beyond such surprises in the recipes, Inglett and Harris inject each post with the vivaciousness and enthusiasm of a best friend who has just gotten incredibly good news. They ask the right questions, provide useful answers, and strike up meaningful conversations. It's impossible to read *The Food Gays* and not smile.

## Q+A

**What is the most treasured item in your kitchen?**
If we had to pick just one, it would be our Urban Cultivator indoor gardening appliance.

**What is your go-to breakfast?**
Eggs—we eat them every day. Either in a wrap or as a frittata.

**What is your go-to cocktail?**
We both usually opt for a Negroni, or its humble cousin the Boulevardier.

**Who would you love to cook for?**
Yotam Ottolenghi. What a fun dinner party that would be!

**Who is your culinary idol?**
The domestic goddess herself, Nigella Lawson. She's the ultimate home cook!

SERVES 2

# ASIAN-STYLE NOODLE BOWLS

## INGREDIENTS

*For the broth*

4 cups (945 ml) water

1 chicken or vegetable bouillon cube

Zest and juice of 1 lemon

1 tablespoon fish sauce

1 teaspoon soy sauce

1 teaspoon toasted sesame oil

⅛ teaspoon ground cinnamon

Salt (optional)

Ground pepper (optional)

7 ounces (200 g) rice noodles

*For the toppings*

Sunflower oil, to cook vegetables

Carrots, thinly sliced

Wild mushrooms, chopped

Bok choy, cut in half lengthwise and sautéed

Gai lan (also known as Chinese broccoli or kale), sautéed

2 large eggs, soft-boiled

Indigo radish microgreens, or other tender greens, for serving

Crispy fried onions

Chili flakes

White sesame seeds

## METHOD

For the broth, in a medium pot, bring the water to a boil. Add the chicken or vegetable bouillon cube, lemon zest and juice, fish sauce, soy sauce, sesame oil, and cinnamon. Season to taste with salt and pepper, if using, and return to a boil. Add the rice noodles and cook, according to the package instructions, until al dente.

To soft boil the eggs, bring a small pot of water to a boil. Gently lower eggs into the water, and cook 6 minutes for a soft, yolky interior, or to desired doneness. Run the eggs under very cold water and peel off the shells. Set aside.

Meanwhile, in a skillet, heat a splash of oil over medium heat. Gently stir-fry your choice of veggies on medium heat until tender, then place them on a parchment-lined baking sheet and keep warm in the oven.

Divide the noodles and broth between 2 bowls and top with the soft-boiled eggs, vegetables, microgreens or greens, crispy onions, chili flakes, and sesame seeds, and serve immediately.

*The best thing about noodle bowls has got to be how customizable they are. Our simple and tasty broth recipe is a great base, and you can top the noodles with whatever toppings you love. We like to add soft-boiled egg and lots of veggies—carrots, wild mushrooms, and Chinese greens such as bok choy and gai lan. We add some crunch with a sprinkle of crispy fried onions, often found in Asian grocery stores.*

# BAKED CONFETTI POTATOES

SERVES
4

## METHOD

Preheat the oven to 400°F (200°C).

Prick the potatoes all over with the tines of a fork, then rub them with the sunflower oil and sprinkle with a little sea salt. Set the potatoes directly on the oven rack and bake for 45 to 55 minutes or until tender.

Use a sharp knife to carefully make a slit down the middle of each potato and season with a pinch of salt and pepper. Top with a good dollop of Greek yogurt, a sprinkle of shredded aged cheddar cheese, and any of the fresh colorful optional toppings. Serve immediately with lime wedges.

## INGREDIENTS

4 sweet or russet potatoes

2 teaspoons sunflower oil

Sea salt, to taste

Ground pepper, to taste

Greek yogurt, for serving

Shredded aged cheddar cheese, for serving

Lime wedges, for serving

*Optional Toppings*

Scallions, thinly sliced

Chives, thinly sliced

Red radishes, trimmed and thinly sliced

Jalapeño or serrano peppers, seeded and thinly sliced

Edamame, shelled and blanched

Fresh or canned corn kernels

Purple cabbage, thinly sliced

Sugar pea microgreens or fresh arugula

Fresh mint leaves, roughly chopped

*When we're exhausted after a long day of photography and food styling, generally the last thing on our minds is what to make for supper. For all intents and purposes, this is the perfect mid-week meal for us when we're low on energy (or enthusiasm), mostly because it requires so little effort and yet yields such impressive results. Enjoy these confetti potatoes all on their own, or alongside a glass of wine and a light side salad.*

Like many others, Valentina Solfrini found vegetarian cooking to be a natural remedy to health problems modern medical science was unable to alleviate. Unlike many others, Solfrini lives on a farm in the Italian countryside. A former graphic designer, Solfrini's moody, nostalgic photography reveals an innate sense of form, color, light, and composition. These are practically fine-art quality prints worthy of a book, and in fact her first book, *Naturally Vegetarian*, will be released in 2017. Fans of *Hortus Cuisine* follow along for Solfrini's luxurious takes on regional Italian cuisine, from the bold (vegetarian) flavors of rustic Tuscan cooking to the handmade pasta shapes of Emilia-Romagna. Solfrini writes philosophically, even poetically, about her life, her passion for farm-to-table cooking, and the everyday delights of living on a farm. She takes inspiration from her surroundings, Asian cuisine, and Renaissance paintings, but mostly showcases straightforward vegetarian fare and sometimes even vegan recipes. She experiments with heirloom seeds, legumes, and grains as well as alternative flours and documents her favorite uses for each in recipes that range from simple to involved, such as Vegan High Protein Hemp and Chickpea Pasta. *Hortus Cuisine* was Editor's Choice for Best New Blog in *Saveur*'s Best Food Blog Awards 2014.

# Hortus Cuisine

**Valentina Solfrini**
Gradara, Italy
www.hortuscuisine.com

---

## Q+A

**What is the most treasured item in your kitchen?**
My Vitamix—a real must-have!

**What is your go-to breakfast?**
Oatmeal with chia seeds, almond milk, and my homemade granola.

**What is your go-to cocktail?**
I do not drink, but my favorite non-alcoholic cocktail has to be a special elderflower spritz they make at a local bar in my town.

**Who would you love to cook for?**
I especially love to cook for those who do not believe vegetarian and vegan food can be tasty—so I can prove them wrong.

**Who is your culinary idol?**
I love Jamie Oliver—the online community he built and his campaign against sugar are so inspiring!

**Name a utensil you can't live without.**
My mortar and pestle, for grinding whole spices and pounding ingredients to a paste.

# HORTUS
# CUISINE

# TAGLIATELLE WITH MUSHROOMS AND TRUFFLES

SERVES 2 TO 3

## METHOD

In a large, heavy skillet, heat the oil and butter over medium heat until the butter is melted. Add the shallots and onion and sauté, stirring occasionally, for 10 minutes or until soft and golden. Add the mixed mushrooms and porcini mushrooms and stir; season to taste with salt and pepper. If using the miso, dissolve it in the hot water then stir it into the sauce. Reduce the heat to medium-low and cook for about 25 minutes or until the water released from the mushrooms has fully evaporated and the flavor is concentrated. If you used dried porcini, add the soaking liquid towards the end of cooking, increase the heat to medium-high, and simmer until the liquid evaporates. Remove from the heat, add the truffle paste or oil, and stir well to combine. For a creamier sauce, purée about ⅓ of the sauce in a blender then pour it back into the pan and stir well to incorporate. Leave the sauce in the skillet and set aside.

Bring a large pot of salted water to a boil and cook the tagliatelle, according to the package instructions, until al dente. Reserve a few tablespoons of the cooking water then drain the tagliatelle.

Place the mushroom sauce over medium heat then add the tagliatelle, along with a tablespoon of the reserved cooking water and cook, stirring, for 2 minutes or until the sauce is creamy. Add the grated cheese, if using, and mix well. Serve immediately with a glass of cold, full-bodied white wine.

## INGREDIENTS

3 tablespoons olive oil

1 tablespoon unsalted butter

2 medium shallots, finely chopped

1 small onion, finely chopped

1 pound (455 g) button and/or champignon mushrooms, thinly sliced

3 medium fresh or frozen porcini mushrooms, chopped (or ¼ cup/20 g dried porcini mushrooms*)

Salt, to taste

Ground pepper, to taste

1 teaspoon white miso (optional)

1 teaspoon hot water

1 heaping teaspoon truffle paste (or 2 teaspoons truffle oil)

1 pound (455 g) fresh whole wheat tagliatelle

½ cup (30 g) grated Parmesan, to finish (optional)

*If using dried porcini, soak them in hot water for at least 1 hour then squeeze to remove the water and finely chop; reserve the soaking liquid.

A classic Italian Sunday lunch dish, this tagliatelle with mushrooms and truffles is a fitting showcase for fall's finest produce. You will need perfect mushrooms for this recipe: button or champignon mushrooms and flavorful porcini. If you can't find fresh porcini, frozen or dried work just as well—when using dried, mind that you must allow time for soaking. You can purchase truffle paste online or in specialty shops, but try to avoid pastes made with summer truffles, also known as Burgundy truffles or Tuber aestivum, as they tend to be bland compared to winter truffles. Truffle oil makes a great substitute or you can skip the truffles altogether—this dish will still be incredibly tasty.

    To make this dish vegan, use egg-free tagliatelle, olive oil instead of butter, and skip the cheese.

# CHAMOMILE-POACHED PLUMS WITH ALMOND CRUMBLE AND CRÉME FRAÎCHE

**SERVES 4 TO 6**

## INGREDIENTS

*For the crème fraîche*

1 cup (240 ml) heavy cream

1 cup (240 ml) buttermilk

½ vanilla bean, split and scraped

1 tablespoon maple syrup or honey

*For the crumble*

⅓ cup (40 g) coconut flour

⅓ cup (50 g) brown rice flour

¼ cup (25 g) almond flour

¼ cup (30 g) tapioca flour

¼ cup (50 g) packed brown sugar

1 teaspoon freshly grated lemon zest

1 teaspoon baking soda

¼ cup (60 ml) milk

3 tablespoons coconut oil, room temperature

1 teaspoon vanilla extract

¼ teaspoon almond extract

2 to 5 tablespoons cold water

## METHOD

For the crème fraîche, combine the heavy cream, buttermilk, and the vanilla bean and seeds in a glass jar and stir well to combine. Cover and let sit at room temperature overnight, or until thickened, making sure to keep the jar out of direct sunlight. Add the maple syrup or honey, and refrigerate a minimum of 2 hours and maximum of 3 to 4 days before using.

For the crumble, in a large bowl, whisk together the coconut, brown rice, almond, and tapioca flours, along with the brown sugar, lemon zest, and baking soda. Add the milk, coconut oil, and the vanilla and almond extracts and stir with a fork until combined. Knead the mixture with your hands, adding cold water by the tablespoonful, until a dough forms. As soon as the dough comes together, knead it for a few more seconds then wrap it tightly in plastic wrap and refrigerate for at least an hour or overnight.

Preheat the oven to 350°F (180°C). Line a baking sheet with parchment paper then lightly oil the parchment with coconut or olive oil.

Using your fingers, break the dough into fine crumbles and spread it evenly in the prepared pan. Bake for 10 to 15 minutes or until golden—mind that the crumble doesn't get too dark.

*I love infusing fruit with floral scents. Chamomile is one of my favorites and plums are its perfect match. I love how the almond flavor in this crumble is reminiscent of Amaretto, a classic Italian liqueur derived from bitter almonds that goes very well with stone fruits of all kinds. Lemon complements this summery dessert with a fragrant accent, while a final touch of crème fraîche adds lusciousness. Plus the crumble is gluten-free, so it's a dessert to fit all needs.*

*If you don't have plums, try making this with peaches or apricots. And, if you want to add an extra kick, finish this with some lilac or lavender salt. To get the best flavor use Italian bitter almonds. If you're not gluten-free, crumble 5 amaretto cookies into the dough for extra flavor and crunch before adding the milk.*

For the plums, combine the chamomile tea, brown sugar, vanilla bean and seeds, and cardamom pods in a deep, wide pot. Bring to a boil then reduce the heat to a gentle simmer. Add the plums, cut-side down, so that they overlap as little as possible, and simmer for 1 minute. Flip the plums over and simmer for 1 more minute—mind that the plums do not get mushy. Use a slotted spoon to carefully transfer the plums to a plate. Return the syrup to a full boil and continue boiling until slightly thickened, about 5 minutes. Pour into a glass jar and let cool in the refrigerator for about 2 hours. While the syrup cools, cover the plums and let come to room temperature or, for a refreshing summer dessert, chill in the refrigerator.

Divide the plums among plates. Top with a dollop of crème fraîche and the crumble, drizzle with the plum syrup, sprinkle with the almond slivers, and serve.

**For the plums**

1½ cups (360 ml) freshly brewed chamomile tea

½ cup (50 g) packed brown sugar

½ vanilla bean, split and scraped

3 to 4 cardamom pods, crushed

1 pound (450 g) plums, halved and pitted

A handful of toasted almond slivers, for serving

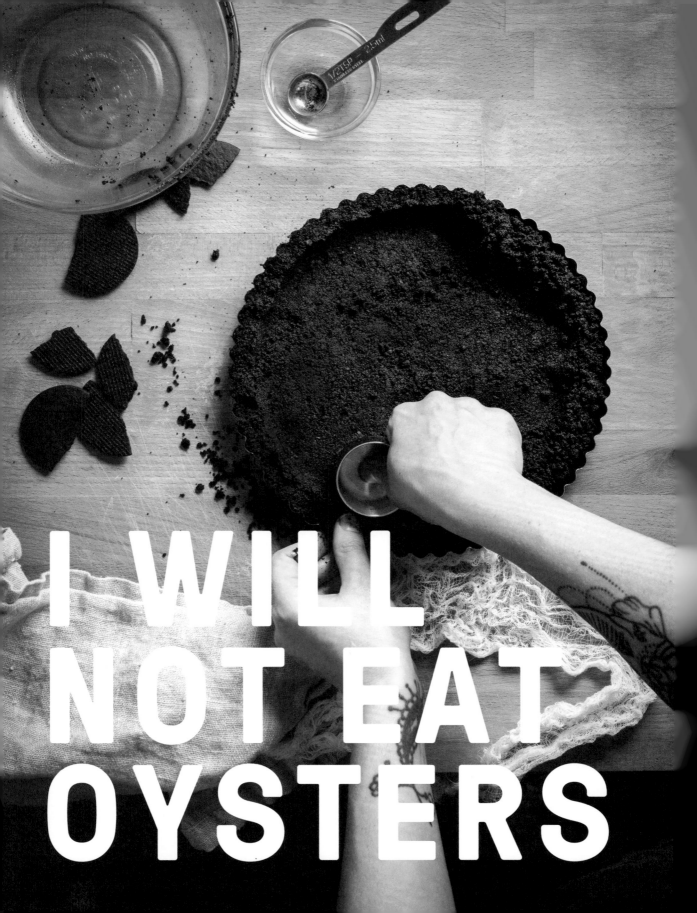

I WILL NOT EAT OYSTERS

# I Will Not Eat Oysters

**Danielle Oron**
Atlanta, Georgia, United States
www.iwillnoteatoysters.com

Atlanta-based Danielle Oron divides her recipes into "the things" (ingredients) and "the way" (instructions)—the kinds of little touches that keep her blog feeling fresh. Her website design, in which one header photo sits atop a trio of complimentary images in each post, is refreshing as well, if only because each image looks so natural, as if captured in a pause between blending ramps into butter when the bright green and golden tones in the butter just happened to look that perfect. Some bloggers teeter into imagery that looks both overstaged and oversaturated; Oron avoids both pitfalls and delivers truly balanced images with eye-catching variations in color, texture, and form. She also balances useful recipe information and kitchen tips with an amusing journal of her daily life. Readers follow along both for the familial updates as well as for new, unique recipe ideas, like Oreo Pretzel Chocolate Salami, Banana Bacon Fat Cornbread, and Pinterest-ready Churro Tater Tots. Oron's Israeli and Moroccan heritage informs many of her dishes, as in Matza Ball Hush Puppies and Overnight Tahini Oats. The classically trained chef—she attended the French Culinary Institute in New York City—writes clear, judicious recipes fit for confident cooks. But her friendly approach encourages anyone to dive into their kitchen. The author of the recently published *Modern Israeli Cooking*, Oron is also a contributor to Yahoo Foods, Pepper Passport, FoodNetwork.ca, and The Nosher.

## Q+A

**What is the most treasured item in your kitchen?**
My hands. They're the best tools I have.

**What is your ultimate comfort food?**
A huge, silky bowl of my mom's feta *cacio e pepe*.

**Name a utensil you can't live without.**
My flat wooden spatula best used for scraping the bottom of a pan when making a sauce.

**What is your go-to breakfast?**
A piece of toast with *labneh*, za'atar, and olive oil.

**Who would you love to cook for?**
Pharrell Williams. Mostly to just watch him eat.

**Who is your culinary idol?**
Gabrielle Hamilton.

# TAHINI DIRTY BLONDIES

## INGREDIENTS

1½ cups (190 g) all-purpose flour

1 teaspoon kosher salt

1 cup (200 g) granulated sugar

½ cup (105 g) light brown sugar

½ cup (110 g) unsalted butter, melted

3 large eggs

1 cup (230 g) tahini

1 teaspoon vanilla bean paste or extract

Black sesame seeds

White sesame seeds

Maldon sea salt

## METHOD

Preheat the oven to 325°F (160°C). Lightly spray an 8-inch (20 cm) square baking pan with cooking spray and line the pan with parchment paper, allowing 1 to 2 inches (2.5 to 5 cm) of parchment to hang over the sides for easy removal.

Sift the flour and salt into a large bowl. In a separate bowl, whisk together the granulated sugar, brown sugar, and butter. Add the eggs, 1 at a time, incorporating each egg before adding the next one, and beat for 2 to 3 minutes or until creamy. Add the tahini and vanilla bean paste or extract and whisk until well combined—mind that you incorporate as little air as possible. Add to the flour mixture and fold until just combined. Scrape the batter into the prepared pan, spreading it evenly. Sprinkle with black and white sesame seeds and bake for 22 to 23 minutes for very gooey blondies or 26 to 28 minutes for blondies that are more cakey. Let cool in pan at least 30 minutes. Use the parchment overhang to lift the blondies from the pan, sprinkle with Maldon sea salt, and cut into 16 pieces. Store in an airtight container for up to 3 days.

*Tahini, a sesame paste used in Middle Eastern cooking, is not only for savory dishes. It's just as perfect in sweets. Halva, for example, is a sesame and sugar treat that's been consumed for centuries all over the region. Tahini is a great alternative to peanut butter, and if you're a first timer, this recipe is an excellent way to introduce it into baked goods. It's nutty, earthy, and adds an intense, deep flavor to pastries.*

*I like blondies a lot more than brownies. I'm actually forbidden from making them at home, because I'll take down a whole tray before they're even cool enough to cut. But when my husband went on a trip for a few days and I was home alone, these tahini dirty blondies happened. They're dirty only because they're not a natural blonde—maybe a blonde with some highlights (and a few low lights.) Looks aside, these blondies are gooey, dense, and creamy. For a nice addition, throw in a handful of semisweet chocolate chips.*

# KANAFEH BAKED BRIE

SERVES
10

## METHOD

Preheat the oven to 350°F (180°C) and line a baking sheet with parchment paper.

Remove the kadaif from the packaging and gently pull it apart with your fingers. Place the kadaif in a large bowl, drizzle with the melted butter, and toss with your hands, until the kadaif is completely coated. Transfer to the lined baking sheet and shape into a circle large enough to wrap around the wheel of Brie.

Arrange ¼ cup (35 g) of the ground walnuts in the center of the kadaif. Place the wheel of Brie on top then sprinkle with the remaining ¼ cup (35 g) ground walnuts, lightly pressing them into the cheese. Wrap the kadaif around the Brie until you have a nice tight bundle. Bake for 35 to 40 minutes or until golden brown.

While the Brie is baking, make the honey syrup: In a small saucepan, combine the honey and water and bring to a gentle simmer over low heat—mind that you don't walk away, as it has a tendency to boil over. Remove from the heat and set aside.

When the Brie comes out of the oven, slowly pour the honey syrup all over it, letting it soak into the pastry. Transfer to a serving dish and garnish with the blackberries and whole walnuts. Serve with baguette crostini and enjoy while the cheese is still hot and melted.

## INGREDIENTS

5½ ounces (155 g) frozen kadaif, thawed

5 tablespoons unsalted butter, melted

½ cup (70 g) finely chopped walnuts, plus more whole walnuts for garnish

1 (6-inch / 15 cm) wheel Brie

⅔ cup (155 ml) honey

½ cup (120 ml) water

Blackberries, for garnish

Toasted baguette slices, for serving

*You've had baklava before. Kanafeh, a cheese pastry soaked in a rose water and honey syrup and topped with ground pistachio, is its close relative. Instead of sheets of phyllo, kanafeh is made with a shredded phyllo-style dough called kadaif. Kanafeh is usually prepared with a slightly salty, stringy cheese to balance the sweet, sticky syrup that soaks into the baked pastry. You'll find kanafeh all over the Middle East, Greece, Turkey, and basically anywhere that was part of the Ottoman Empire. This is why there are different spellings and pronunciations. For example, kadaif is spelled kataifi in Greece. But enough with the culture lesson.*

*Growing up in an affluent Jersey suburb, there was baked Brie at every dinner party I was dragged to by my parents. It was wrapped in store-bought piecrust, topped with some sort of fruit, and never made with real authentic French Brie, so I didn't really understand it, nor did I ever try it. I'll take a plain cracker, thanks. As an adult, hosting my own dinner parties, I thought I'd give it a try after all those years of running away from it. Obviously, I had to give it my own twist. This recipe combines my American upbringing with my Middle Eastern roots. I think it works perfectly together. It's almost as if it's a reflection of myself. (Sorry, got a bit deep there.)*

Prerna and Abhishek Singh are the photogenic couple who turned a casual food blog into a social media community seemingly overnight. Thanks to Abhishek's tech savvy and Prerna's kitchen skills, the site is a resource for cooks who can also contribute their own tips, tricks, and recipes thanks to a user interface that allows readers to create an account and interact with other cooks. Prerna's cuisine focuses on North Indian fare: Tomato-based curries, rotis, lentils, and a wide range of vegetables star in recipes for breakfast, lunch, and dinner. Because the couple have two young daughters, kid-friendly recipes are on offer here too, including ones that bridge the gap between traditional Indian recipes and American mainstays (think: naan pizza). Adorable stories about the children's lives and tastes make for fun recipe introductions. Interspersed throughout the blog are 101-type guides on American basics like mashed potatoes, French toast, and scrambled eggs, along with Indian favorites like cilantro chutney, caramelized onions, and *dosas*. But it's really Prerna's mastery of Indian spices that makes *Indian Simmer* a must-read. She knows how to layer flavors and build upon them in one pot, coaxing the sweetness from onions before adding chilies for heat. Learn techniques like *dum pukht*, or how to layer rice and vegetables such that they cook in their own moisture; and specialties like *jalebi*, a fermented yogurt-based fritter served soaked in sugar syrup for dessert. *Indian Simmer* has been featured on the Food Network, in the *Guardian* and *Food & Wine* magazine, and was named the Editor's Choice for Best Regional Blog in *Saveur* Best Food Blog Awards 2014.

# Indian Simmer

**Prerna and Abhishek Singh**
San Francisco Bay Area, California, United States
www.indiansimmer.com

## Q+A

**What is the most treasured item in your kitchen?**
My mortar and pestle. My mum put it in my suitcase ten years back when I moved to the United States.

**What is your ultimate comfort food?**
My dad's chicken curry paired with hot puffed rotis straight off the stove.

**Name a utensil you can't live without.**
My Microplane grater. I use it to grate ginger or whole spices to go into my chai pot. I cannot live without that spiced chai and that grater is a lifesaver!

**What is your go-to cocktail?**
I'm more of a wine person, but I can't say no to the Mojitos my husband makes.

**Who would you love to cook for?**
My late grandma who is a huge inspiration in my life, a feisty young widow who raised a large family all by herself. And she was a hell of a cook.

**Who is your culinary idol?**
If I cannot pick my mum or my mother-in-law, then it would be Ms. Madhur Jaffrey, the Julia Child of Indian cuisine!

# INDIAN SIMMER

# READER FAVORITE
# NAAN

MAKES
6 TO 8
NAAN

## METHOD

In a large bowl, whisk together the flour, sugar, baking powder, baking soda, and salt. In a small bowl, whisk together the milk and yogurt. Slowly stir the milk-yogurt mixture into the flour mixture. Gently bring the ingredients together until just combined. On a large table or countertop, knead the mixture until it comes together into a soft and pliable dough. Add a little water if needed. Form the dough into a ball and place in a lightly oiled large bowl. Cover with a tea towel and let rise in a dark, warm, dry place for 3 to 4 hours or until more than doubled in size.

When the dough has doubled in size, punch it down then take it out of the bowl and knead it for about 1 minute. Return the dough to the bowl, cover with a tea towel and let rise for 45 to 60 minutes or until doubled in size and studded with small air pockets.

Dust a large table or countertop with flour. Knead the dough for 3 to 5 minutes or until it is smooth and comes together in a ball. Divide the dough into 6 to 8 small balls. Use a rolling pin to roll the balls out into slightly thick, preferably teardrop-shaped, flatbreads.

Heat a heavy pan or wok with a lid over medium-high heat.

Sprinkle one side of the flatbread with nigella seeds, chopped cilantro, chopped onion, or minced garlic. Brush the other side with water. Once the pan is very hot, add 1 flatbread, wet-side down, and cover with a lid. Cook for about 30 seconds or until bubbles appear on the surface. Turn a nearby burner on high heat. Use tongs to carefully flip the flatbread and place directly over the open flame. Cook for about 30 to 45 seconds or until charred brown spots appear. Repeat with the remaining flatbreads. Serve immediately.

## INGREDIENTS

3 cups (390 g) all-purpose flour, plus more for dusting

½ tablespoon granulated sugar

¾ teaspoon baking powder

½ teaspoon baking soda

¼ teaspoon salt

½ cup (120 ml) warm whole or 2% milk

½ cup (120 g) plain yogurt, preferably whole milk

½ tablespoon canola or olive oil, for oiling the bowl

Water

Nigella seeds, for topping

Chopped cilantro, for topping

Chopped onion, for topping

Finely chopped garlic, for topping

*Naan, khamiri, or nan, one of the most beloved varieties of Indian bread, is a leavened flatbread that's baked in a traditional stone oven called a tandoor. While most Indian breads are made with durum wheat flour (or aata), naan is commonly made with all-purpose flour. The dough is fermented with yeast or a combination of yogurt and milk, and, in some modern variations, with the addition of baking soda or powder. Following fermentation, rounds of dough are slapped onto the inside walls of a hot tandoor and once the naan is cooked through, it automatically releases itself from the tandoor. Not everyone is lucky enough to own a full-fledged tandoor, but no human should be denied the pleasure of homemade naan! This recipe allows naan lovers to make restaurant-style naan in the comfort of their own kitchen.*

# NEW RECIPE
# RUSTIC CARAMELIZED ONION, FETA, AND PEAR GALETTE

**SERVES 2 TO 3**

## INGREDIENTS

*For the crust*

1¼ cups (160 g) all-purpose flour, plus more for dusting

½ cup (115 g) unsalted butter, cold and cut into small pieces

½ teaspoon salt

About ¼ cup (60 ml) ice-cold water

*For the caramelized onions*

2 to 3 tablespoons olive oil or butter

3 cups sliced yellow onions (about 3 medium onions)

1 teaspoon granulated sugar

½ teaspoon salt

1 tablespoon balsamic or red wine vinegar

*For the galette*

1 firm, ripe bosc pear, cored and thinly sliced

⅓ to ½ cup (about 2 ounces / 55 g) crumbled feta

Salt

Ground pepper

1 large egg

2 to 3 tablespoons water

Fresh mint leaves, for garnish

## METHOD

For the crust, combine the flour, butter, and salt in a food processor. Pulse several times to cut the butter into the flour until there are only small pieces left. Slowly add the ice-cold water, 1 tablespoon at a time, pulsing just until the dough comes together.

Transfer the dough to a lightly floured table or countertop. Use your hands to gather the dough together then gently knead until it forms a soft, smooth ball. Use a rolling pin to roll out into a disc slightly larger than 9 inches (23 cm) in diameter. Wrap the disc tightly in plastic wrap and refrigerate until ready to use, at least 45 minutes and up to a week.

For the caramelized onions, in a large, heavy (preferably not nonstick) pan, heat the oil or butter over medium heat. Add the onions, stir to coat them in the oil or butter, and then reduce the heat to medium-low. Slowly cook the onions, stirring every 10 to 15 minutes—mind that the onions are browning but not burning. After about 20 minutes, add the sugar and salt then continue cooking for 35 to 40 minutes or until the onions are soft and golden with some brown pieces stuck to the bottom of the pan. Add the vinegar to deglaze the pan, using a spatula to scrape any bits and pieces off the bottom.

Preheat the oven to 400°F (200°C). Line a baking sheet with parchment paper.

For the galette, place the disc of dough on the lined baking sheet. Spread the caramelized onions on top, leaving a 1 to 1½-inch (2.5 to 4 cm) border. Arrange the pear slices in a thin layer on top of the onions and sprinkle with the feta. Fold up the edge of the dough and gently press it into the onions and pears, creating a pleated border. Season to taste with salt and pepper.

*Sweet caramelized onions, feta, and delicate baked pears are a match made in heaven. In this savory galette, all of those flavors are wrapped in buttery, flaky pastry that melts in your mouth and adds just the right hint of salt. Fresh mint lends brightness and a lovely shot of color.*

In a small bowl, beat together the egg and water. Brush the egg wash over the folded border of the galette. Bake for 40 to 45 minutes or until the crust is golden and the cheese is melted and bubbling. Garnish with mint and serve.

# KALUHI'S KITCHEN

# Kaluhi's Kitchen

**Kaluhi Adagala**
Nairobi, Kenya
www.kaluhiskitchen.com

Kaluhi Adagala, the force behind *Kaluhi's Kitchen*, says her site is a Kenyan food blog for the everyday Kenyan. This means she's using only ingredients readily available in Kenya. Because she's pressed for time, she also wanted to present recipes that streamlined the home cooking process. In this way, *Kaluhi's Kitchen* has something for everyone across the globe and provides a delicious look into the modern Kenyan kitchen. Adagala doesn't do much baking—the blog is focused on the savory side of the kitchen—but she does dabble in sweet side dishes, such as Crispy Sweet Potatoes with Orange Rosemary Syrup, and for breakfast, Coconut and Chocolate Chip Drop Scones. Reviews of local restaurants and food festivals are interspersed among recipes like Ginger Matoke Masala, Sweet and Spicy Chicken Wings, Mango Mint Salad with Passion Fruit Syrup, and Mbuzi Meatball Mshikaki, which are goat meatball skewers seasoned with garam masala, ginger, garlic, and barbecue sauce, and would be great made with any meat and served as an appetizer or main course. A natural storyteller, Adagala has led delighted fans along a mouthwatering journey of kitchen experiments, and she has been rewarded with a very vibrant comment community in a decidedly convivial atmosphere. *Kaluhi's Kitchen* was the 2016 winner of Kenya's Blog Awards.

## Q+A

**What is the most treasured item in your kitchen?**
Steel stove.

**What is your ultimate comfort food?**
Fresh custard with warm vanilla and poppy seed cake.

**What is your go-to breakfast?**
Tea, scrambled eggs in ghee, eight-grain whole wheat bread.

**What is your go-to cocktail?**
Loquat reduction, fresh sage, ginger, brandy, limes.

**Who would you love to cook for?**
Orie Rogo Manduli.

**Who is your culinary idol?**
Siba Mtongana.

# READER FAVORITE
# GINGER MATOKE MASALA

## INGREDIENTS

Vegetable oil

1 teaspoon cumin seeds

1 cup (150 g) finely chopped red onion

½ green bell pepper, finely diced

½ tablespoon minced fresh ginger

1 tomato, finely chopped

2 tablespoons tomato paste

1½ tablespoons garlic powder

1 tablespoon ground coriander

½ teaspoon turmeric

½ teaspoon paprika

½ cup (120 ml) hot vegetable broth or water

Salt

Ground pepper

4 large matoke, peels still green, or raw plantains

Onion, chives, and cilantro, for serving

## METHOD

In a medium sized pan, heat a splash of vegetable oil over medium-high heat. Add the cumin seeds and toast for 1 to 2 minutes or until fragrant. Add the onion, bell pepper, and ginger, reduce the heat to medium-low and cook for about 4 minutes or until the onion has softened. Add the tomato, tomato paste, garlic powder, coriander, turmeric, and paprika and stir until well combined, then add the hot vegetable broth or water and stir again. Season to taste with salt and pepper. Reduce the heat to low and cook for 10 to 15 minutes.

While the masala sauce is cooking, peel the matoke and cover with cold salted water in a large pot. Bring to a boil and continue boiling for 8 minutes until just tender. Remove them from the heat, cut the matoke lengthwise into thin slices, add them to the masala sauce, and stir gently to combine. Continue to cook on low for 5 to 8 minutes so the matoke can absorb all the flavors. Garnish with onion, chives, and cilantro and serve.

*Growing up, I never liked matoke (also known as cooking bananas) despite my mom cooking them every fortnight. She created various recipes to get us to love them, and with time, we did! Over the years, I played around with different matoke dishes and while we enjoyed many of them, this is by far my favorite.*

*Matoke are in the same family as plantain but do not have the same characteristics. Matoke are starchier, not as sweet, and have to be cooked when the peel is still green to achieve the desired taste when stewed.*

# ROAST CHICKEN IN SWEET CHILI SAUCE (KUKU CHOMA)

SERVES 4

## METHOD

Prepare a grill (or grill pan) to cook over high heat at 390°F (200°C).

For the rub, in a small bowl, whisk together the olive oil, garlic powder, onion powder, pepper, and paprika.

In a medium bowl, pour the wet rub over the chicken drumsticks and toss to coat. Grill the drumsticks, along with the rosemary, for 5 to 7 minutes or until the chicken is just cooked through. Discard the rosemary and set the chicken aside to rest.

In a medium skillet, heat a splash of vegetable oil over medium-high heat. Add the green onion, garlic, and ginger and sauté for 2 to 4 minutes until the onions are soft and fragrant. Add the hot water, tomato, brown sugar, tomato paste, soy sauce, cayenne pepper, and ground pepper and cook for 8 minutes. Add the green bell pepper, reduce the heat to medium-low, and cook for 10 to 15 minutes or until the sauce thickens. Add the chicken, toss to coat in the sauce, and cook for 2 to 3 minutes or until the chicken is warmed through. Season to taste with salt and serve with freshly cooked rice.

## INGREDIENTS

*For the wet rub*

3 tablespoons olive oil

1½ tablespoons garlic powder

1½ tablespoons onion powder

1 tablespoon ground pepper

½ teaspoon paprika

*For the chicken*

4 chicken drumsticks

1 sprig rosemary

Vegetable oil

½ cup (20 g) finely chopped green onion

4 cloves garlic, finely chopped

½ tablespoon finely chopped fresh ginger

½ cup (120 ml) hot water

1 tomato, finely diced

2 tablespoons dark brown sugar

1 tablespoon tomato paste

1 tablespoon light mushroom or regular soy sauce

½ tablespoon cayenne pepper

½ teaspoon ground pepper

¼ cup finely chopped green bell pepper

Salt

*When food and* choma *are in the same sentence, it usually refers to something roasted, especially roasted meat. Kenyans love everything "choma" and you always find plenty of roasted meat of different kinds at any social gathering. Kuku choma,* which is roast chicken, *is my favorite roasted meat. I put my own twist on my favorite Kenyan roast and add a rich sweet chili sauce that complements the mild smokiness of the meat.*

*Kuku choma is often served with pilau, a spiced fragrant rice dish cooked in seasoned broth, originally from the coastal areas of Kenya. Plain basmati rice may be used as a substitute.*

# Krautkopf

**Yannic Schon & Susann Probst**
Berlin, Germany
www.kraut-kopf.de

Berlin-based photographers and writers Susann Probst and Yannic Schon seek not to simply highlight recipes on their inspiring blog, but to shine a light on gatherings and the sorts of dishes that are best shared with others. "Kraut kopf" means "head of cabbage" in German, so, yes, classic German recipes (written in both German and English) are featured, but Probst and Schon are redefining classic German cuisine, which tends to be meat-heavy, by focusing on vegetarian recipes. Hearty root vegetables, dark leafy greens, and, yes, cabbage are transformed, gently, into dishes that look like they came out of the kitchen of a fine dining restaurant. Pumpkins are roasted and stuffed with lentils; peas and pistachios form a ravioli filling; and elderflower perfumes a classy white cheesecake. Sometimes a simpler dish like a vegetable-filled crepe-like pancake (Gratin Pancake) is turned on its head and buried under a brûléed cap of cheese and sauce. Recipes are helpfully arranged by season and diet, and a basics section covers sauces, curry paste, non-dairy milks, doughs, and stocks. The pair's inventiveness is only trumped by their delightful photography. Designed to give the viewer—whether reading on mobile, desktop, or tablet—a book-like experience, the photographs are blown up almost to the width of the page, and are so crisp that the reader might be tempted to reach up and flip the page or dog-ear a corner. It's no wonder then that *Krautkopf* won Best-Designed Blog in *Saveur* Blog '15 Awards, or that they published their own cookbook in 2015 called *Krautkopf: Vegetarisch kochen und genießen* (Seasonal Vegetarian Recipes).

---

## Q+A

**What is the most treasured item in your kitchen?**
Mortar and pestle.

**What is your ultimate comfort food?**
Any type of curry.

**Name a utensil you can't live without.**
Camera.

**What is your go-to breakfast?**
Pancakes with berries and granola.

**What is your go-to cocktail?**
Moscow mule with homemade ginger beer.

**Who would you love to cook for?**
Everyone who would like to taste our food.

# KRAUTKOPF

# THAI COCONUT SOUP

SERVES 2

## METHOD

Place the tofu in a resealable container or plastic bag. In a small bowl, combine ⅓ cup plus 2 tablespoons (100 ml) of the vegetable stock with 1 tablespoon of the curry paste and whisk until the curry paste is dissolved. Pour over the tofu, cover, and refrigerate overnight—from time to time, shake the container to make sure the marinade covers the tofu on all sides.

The next day, heat the coconut oil in a large, heavy pot over medium-high heat. Add the remaining 2 teaspoons curry paste and cook for 2 to 3 minutes. Add the remaining vegetable stock and bring to a boil. Use the back of a chef's knife to pound the lemongrass, so that the fibers open and emit their flavor. Add the lemongrass, along with the kaffir lime leaves, to the stock and reduce to a simmer.

While the stock simmers, cook the rice noodles: Bring a large pot of water to a boil, remove from the heat, and add the rice noodles. Let the noodles cook, according to the package instructions, until al dente, then rinse with cold water. Set aside.

To fry the tofu, heat the vegetable oil in a small, heavy pot over medium-high heat. Take the tofu out of the marinade and pat dry with paper towels. When the oil is hot, carefully place the tofu in the oil and deep fry, occasionally turning with a slotted ladle or spoon, for 5 minutes or until golden. Transfer to paper towels to drain. Cut the tofu into thin slices.

Add the tofu, along with the shiitake mushrooms and coconut milk, to the soup and simmer for another 10 minutes. Season to taste with lime juice and salt. Divide the rice noodles between 2 bowls and top with the soup. Serve immediately with the spinach, mung bean sprouts, green onion, herbs, peanuts, and lime wedges.

## INGREDIENTS

9 ounces (250 g) organic firm tofu, cut in half

4 cups (950 ml) vegetable stock

1 tablespoon plus 2 teaspoons red curry paste

1 teaspoon virgin coconut oil

1 stalk lemongrass

2 kaffir lime leaves

4½ ounces (125 g) rice noodles

About 2 cups or ½ liter vegetable oil, for frying

3½ ounces (100 g) shiitake mushrooms, thinly sliced

1 cup (250 ml) coconut milk

Juice of ½ lime, plus wedges for serving

Fine sea salt

1 handful baby spinach leaves

1 handful mung bean sprouts

1 green onion, thinly sliced

Fresh herbs, such as cilantro, mint, Thai basil, celery greens, and shiso

Toasted peanuts, roughly chopped

*We love Asian cuisine, especially for its use of fresh and exotic herbs. We prefer to serve this soup with only rice noodles, tofu, and mushrooms and to arrange an extra plate for the spinach, bean sprouts, green onion, fresh herbs, peanuts, and lime wedges. This way, everyone can garnish their soup as they like.*

*Tofu is mild, so we like to give it some much needed bang by marinating it in a curry paste mixture overnight. This means you'll need to start this recipe a day ahead.*

## INGREDIENTS

*For the falafel*

5 ounces (150 g) dried chickpeas

5 ounces (150 g) fresh shelled fava beans

1 shallot, finely chopped

1 to 2 cloves garlic, finely chopped

½ bunch flat-leaf parsley, leaves only

3 to 4 sprigs fresh cilantro, leaves only

1 teaspoon freshly squeezed lemon juice

1 teaspoon cumin seeds, crushed with a mortar and pestle

½ teaspoon coriander seeds, crushed with a mortar and pestle

½ teaspoon ground sumac

½ teaspoon baking soda

Fine sea salt

About 1 quart (1 L) vegetable oil, for frying

*For the salad*

3 tablespoons raspberry balsamic vinegar

1 tablespoon olive oil

1 teaspoon Dijon mustard

1 teaspoon rice syrup or ½ teaspoon maple syrup

Fine sea salt

Ground pepper

4¼ ounces (120 g) baby lettuce and wild herbs

5¼ ounces (150 g) blackberries

# WILD HERB SALAD WITH FAVA BEAN FALAFEL

## METHOD

For the falafel, soak the chickpeas overnight in plenty of cold water. The next day, thoroughly rinse the chickpeas and let them drain well (they won't be cooked for this dish).

Bring a small pot of salted water to a boil and blanch the fava beans for about 5 minutes or until the white skins begin to split. Drain and quickly rinse with cold water. Slip off the white skins and discard.

Combine the chickpeas, fava beans, shallot, garlic, parsley, cilantro, lemon juice, cumin, coriander, sumac, and baking soda in a food processor and pulse until the mixture has a medium-fine texture— mind that you don't grind the mixture too finely or the falafel will be dense rather than soft and fluffy. Season to taste with salt. Form the mixture into ping-pong-size balls.

To fry the falafel, heat the vegetable oil in a large, heavy pot over medium-high heat. When the oil is hot, carefully place falafel in the oil and deep fry, occasionally turning them with a slotted ladle or spoon, for about 5 minutes or until golden brown. Transfer to paper towels to drain. Bring the oil back up to temperature and fry the remaining falafel. Place the falafel in the oven to keep warm, if desired.

For the salad, in a small bowl, whisk together the vinegar, olive oil, mustard, and rice syrup. Season to taste with salt and pepper.

In a large bowl, toss together the baby lettuce, wild herbs, and blackberries. Drizzle with the dressing, top with the falafel, and serve immediately.

*When talking about our favorite dishes, we can't forget versatile falafel. Falafel is ideal for eating on the go, big appetites, or when combined with a wild herb salad, perfect for a light dinner.*

*The dried chickpeas need to be soaked overnight, so be sure to start the recipe a day ahead.*

*For the salad dressing, we use raspberry balsamic vinegar because it is very fruity, thick, and not as sour as regular fruit vinegars. When using one of those, you might have to balance the sourness with more syrup.*

In general, food bloggers seem to live charmed lives, but few enjoy the life Saghar Setareh of *Lab Noon* has created for herself. After growing up in the Iranian capital of Tehran, she immigrated to Rome to study graphic design, and, like many before her, fell in love with the city, its culture, and its cuisine. Despite the affinity she felt for her newfound home, Setareh continued to miss Iran. The blog became a way for her to stay connected to her past while building a home in an entirely new place. In addition to recipes, Setareh peppers the blog with DIY projects—like jarred pomegranate gin with cardamom and cloves—and has used the space as a sort of experimental design studio. Her choices in typography and graphical elements verge on the playful, lending a tender note to memories of her youth and musings on home. Though she started the blog in 2014, thanks to inventive flavor combinations and gorgeous photography, fans keep coming back for more. In particular, Setareh shows a knack for infusing Italian dishes with traditional Persian flavors, like setting the dark leafy greens used in Iranian fritters or stews known collectively as *ghormeh sabzi* in a frittata, or adding tiny Persian lentils to a risotto. Or try her take on olive oil ricotta cake, popular in the south of Italy, infused with the flavor of orange blossom water, a sophisticated floral finish for a cake rooted in tradition. A *Saveur* Blog '15 Awards finalist for Best Special Interest Blog, *Lab Noon* is written in both Italian and English.

# Lab Noon

Saghar Setareh
Rome, Italy
www.labnoon.com

---
## Q+A
---

**What is the most treasured item in your kitchen?**
High-quality Iranian saffron and my seeds (nigella, sesame, Iranian chia seeds), which I use daily, mostly in breakfast.

**What is your ultimate comfort food?**
A salad! Whenever I have no time or idea about what to cook or eat I make salads. I mix and match the most unexpected ingredients—cooked and raw veggies, grains, seeds and nuts, fruit—and the meal is sorted.

**Name a utensil you can't live without.**
My tiny strainer that I use for draining everything. And a pair of kitchen tongs.

**What is your go-to breakfast?**
Traditional rolled oats! Soaked overnight, made into a single pancake or good ol' porridge, I can't not have my oats for breakfast (topped with fruit and seeds and nuts).

**Who is your culinary idol?**
Jamie Oliver. He evoked the foodie in me. I love his rustic, homey cooking style. His determination to change the food habits of the world, especially those of school kids, is so inspirational.

# LAB
# NOON

# FRAGRANT RICOTTA CAKE

SERVES 8

## METHOD

Preheat the oven to 350°F (180°C). Butter a round 8-inch (20 cm) pan.

For the cake, use an electric mixer to beat the ricotta in a medium bowl until smooth. Add the muscovado sugar and continue beating until the mixture is smooth and caramel colored. Add the lemon zest and orange blossom water. Add the eggs, 1 at a time, incorporating each egg before adding the next one, and beat until well combined and pale. Add the olive oil. Beat until the mixture is smooth.

In a large bowl, sift together the bread and spelt flours, adding any bran that remains in the sifter to the bowl. Add the almond flour, baking powder, and salt, and mix well. Gradually and gently fold the flour mixture into the ricotta mixture until well combined—if you mix too roughly, the cake will lose its airy texture. Scrape the batter into the prepared pan and bake for 20 to 30 minutes or until golden. If you insert a skewer in the middle of the cake it should come out clean. Let the cake cool completely on a rack before turning out onto a plate.

For the frosting, use a wooden spoon to stir the ricotta in a medium bowl until smooth. Gradually add the maple syrup to taste, beating until incorporated. Add the orange blossom water and beat until smooth. Cover and refrigerate until the cake has cooled.

To assemble the cake, use a spatula and circular movements to spread the frosting all over the top and sides of the cake and sprinkle with the pistachios on all sides.

## INGREDIENTS

*For the cake*

9 ounces (250 g) ricotta, preferably sheep's milk

¾ cup (150 g) muscovado sugar

Freshly grated zest of 1 lemon

½ teaspoon orange blossom water

3 large eggs

¼ cup (60 ml) olive oil

¾ cup plus 1 tablespoon (100 g) whole wheat bread flour

⅓ cup plus 1 tablespoon (50 g) wholegrain spelt flour

¾ cup (70 g) almond flour

½ teaspoon baking powder

Pinch of salt

*For the frosting*

9 ounces (250 g) ricotta, preferably sheep's milk

3 tablespoons maple syrup, or to taste

½ teaspoon orange blossom water

3 tablespoons (30 g) pistachios, toasted and finely chopped

*This cake was inspired by pastiera, a Neapolitan cake filled with wheat-berries, ricotta, and the perfume of fresh citrus and orange blossom water. Almond flour—just ground almonds—makes the texture rich. It's an elegant and delicate cake yet has a homemade and rustic feel to it.*

# SPICY ROASTED CHICKPEA SALAD WITH GREEN APPLES

SERVES 2

## INGREDIENTS

*For the roasted chickpeas*

1½ cups (280 g) drained and rinsed canned chickpeas

2 tablespoons olive oil

1 small clove garlic, grated

2 teaspoons ground turmeric

1 teaspoon ground cumin

1 teaspoon ground sumac

½ teaspoon cayenne pepper

Salt

*For the tahini-honey dressing*

½ teaspoon freshly grated ginger root

Juice of 1 small lemon

2 teaspoons tahini

1 teaspoon honey

1 teaspoon olive oil

Pinch of salt

*For the salad*

Half a small head of radicchio, leaves separated

1 handful seasonal greens, such as baby spinach

1 green apple, cut into wedges

2 heaping tablespoons (20 g) hazelnuts, toasted and roughly chopped

## METHOD

Preheat the oven to 350°F (180°C). Line a baking sheet with parchment paper.

For the roasted chickpeas, in a medium bowl, toss together the chickpeas, olive oil, garlic, turmeric, cumin, sumac, and cayenne. Season to taste with salt. Spread onto the lined baking sheet and bake, occasionally shaking the pan, for about 20 minutes or until the chickpeas are crisp.

For the tahini-honey dressing, in a small bowl, whisk together the ginger, lemon juice, tahini, honey, olive oil, and salt.
Set aside.

For the salad, arrange the radicchio and greens on a large platter and place the apple wedges on top. Sprinkle with the hazelnuts and roasted chickpeas, drizzle with the dressing, and serve.

*This salad is best made in early fall, when apples are super crunchy and a little sour. Although it's made with flavors and spices from the Middle East, the overall taste is very international.*

# LADY
# AND PUPS

# Lady and Pups-an angry food blog

**Mandy Lee**
Hong Kong
www.ladyandpups.com

Mandy Lee is angry. She has been angry, chiefly, about living in Beijing—though the lady and her pups have relocated to Hong Kong—about the politics and policies there, and about her sense of helplessness about the whole thing. But readers have been following along for six years and counting because the spirited blogger channels her anger into whip-smart writing and detailed recipes driven by a search to create something new that's also grounded in memory and history. Known for inventive riffs on international dishes, Lee's blog has earned its share of Internet acclaim (it was featured in *Saveur's* "Sites We Love" series in 2013). Recipes like Spicy Cured Yolk Rice Bowl, Pumpkin Spice Coconut Ice Cream in a Blanket, and Crusty Radish Dumplings for My Dumpling bend the minds of even experienced cooks, but it's her inventive takes on baked goods that have excited readers most. Pasta machine cruffins, for instance, turn standard pastry practices on their proverbial little heads. Rather than rolling and folding butter into laminated dough, Lee runs the dough through a pasta machine on the thinnest setting, butters each side of the flattened dough, and then rolls up the dough into a log that she twists into a semi-knot. This dough turns into the many-layered crust for the Portuguese tart known as *pastel de nata*. In 2012 she published a post called "The Dreamiest of Dreamy Milk Toast," and the photos of the finished, nearly pearlescent loaf of bread flew across the Internet. (Secrets in that recipe include the use of sweetened condensed milk and browned butter.) Now that Lee has left Beijing for Hong Kong, will she be as angry and obsessed with perfection? Will she still delight readers with recipes like Sticky Toffee Pancakes? One thing's for sure: she'll always have those pups.

---

## Q+A

**What is the most treasured item in your kitchen?**
Curiosity seasoned with just the right amount of unrealistic optimism.

**What is your ultimate comfort food?**
Really mushy and room-temperature instant ramen.

**What is your go-to breakfast?**
Coffee and procrastination.

**Who would you love to cook for?**
My future army of French bulldogs.

**Who is your culinary idol?**
Anthony Bourdain, but I'm pretty sure he's a lousy cook.

# MY SPICY FRIED CHICKEN SANDWICH

SERVES 4

## INGREDIENTS

*For the chicken and brine*

½ cup (125 ml) pickling juice from canned pickled jalapeños

¼ small onion, grated

1 teaspoon freshly grated ginger

¾ teaspoon salt

½ teaspoon granulated sugar

¼ teaspoon ground pepper

4 skinless, boneless chicken thighs

*For the jalapeño-yogurt mayo*

½ cup (105 g) mayonnaise

½ cup (125 g) plain full-fat Greek yogurt

½ cup (85 g) canned pickled jalapeños, drained and finely chopped

2 tablespoons finely chopped onion

2 tablespoons finely chopped green onion

½ teaspoon ground pepper

Salt

*For frying the chicken*

½ cup (65 g) cornstarch

¼ teaspoon ground pepper

Canola oil, for frying

¼ cup (30 g) all-purpose flour

2 tablespoons panko breadcrumbs

2 teaspoons cayenne pepper, plus more to taste

## METHOD

For the chicken and brine, combine the pickling juice, onion, ginger, salt, sugar, and pepper in a medium bowl and whisk to combine. Add the chicken, cover, and refrigerate for at least 4 hours and up to 8 hours.

For the jalapeño-yogurt mayo, combine the mayonnaise, yogurt, jalapeños, onion, green onion, and pepper in a small airtight container and whisk to combine. Season to taste with salt, cover, and refrigerate until ready to use.

To fry the chicken, in a shallow bowl, season the cornstarch with ¼ teaspoon of ground pepper.

Remove the chicken from the brine and pat with paper towels to remove any excess brine. Dredge the chicken thighs, 1 at a time, in the cornstarch—mind that they're evenly coated—and tap gently to remove any excess. Place on a rack and set aside.

Heat 4 inches of canola oil in a large, heavy pot over medium-high heat.

In a shallow bowl, whisk together the flour, panko breadcrumbs, cayenne and white pepper, garlic powder, salt, baking soda, and ½ teaspoon pepper. Add the ice-cold water, Sriracha, and rice vinegar, and stir with a fork just until a slightly lumpy batter comes together. Dip the chicken thighs, 1 at a time, into the batter—mind that they're completely coated.

*What would I change, I asked myself, if I were to recreate a classic fried chicken sandwich? There are basic premises that I would keep: the soft potato rolls, the Southern-style batter-frying, the tangy cool dressing. Then, I would introduce an additional element of kicks. First, a tart and spicy brine for the chicken, and second, a frying batter made with Sriracha sauce.*

*It's big. It's guilt-filled. It shatters in between bites, so all the juices flow through, savory and tangy, hot and cool at the same time. You'll probably need a nap after this, during which you'll dream about having another chicken sandwich.*

*It's important to allow 4 to 6 hours for the brining to get the maximum juiciness.*

When the oil is hot enough, use tongs to carefully dip 1 chicken thigh in the oil, swirling it for about 15 seconds or until the batter is firm, and then releasing it into the oil. Fry until the chicken is golden brown and crispy, turning each piece about halfway through cooking. Transfer to a rack to drain, and immediately season with ground white pepper and cayenne, if you want more heat. Repeat with the remaining chicken thighs—mind that the oil stays hot enough.

To serve, spread a generous amount of jalapeño-yogurt mayo on each side of a sliced potato roll. Toss the shredded lettuce with just enough jalapeño-yogurt mayo to lightly coat then divide the mixture among the bottom buns. Arrange a piece of fried chicken on each sandwich and finish with the top buns. Serve immediately.

2 teaspoons ground white pepper, plus more to taste

1 teaspoon garlic powder

½ teaspoon salt

⅛ teaspoon baking soda

½ teaspoon ground pepper

¼ cup plus 2 teaspoons (70 ml) ice-cold water

¼ cup (70 g) Sriracha sauce, preferably cold

2 teaspoons rice vinegar

4 potato rolls, split, for serving

Shredded lettuce, for serving

## INGREDIENTS

*For the shrimp toast*

7½ ounces (210 grams) medium, shell-on tiger shrimp (about 18 shrimp)

1½ ounces (45 grams) ground pork

1 large egg white

1 teaspoon freshly grated ginger

½ teaspoon fish sauce

¼ teaspoon ground white pepper

8 slices white bread

Melted butter, for grilling

12 slices provolone or Gouda

Fresh chives, finely chopped

*For the broth*

Shrimp shells (reserved from above)

2 stalks lemongrass, roughly chopped with tough outer layer removed

6 fresh kaffir lime leaves

2 cloves garlic, peeled

2 Asian or small shallots, peeled

2 large, fresh red chiles

1 tablespoon freshly grated galangal (or 2 tablespoons freshly grated ginger)

1 tablespoon coconut oil

1¾ cups (420 ml) coconut milk

1¾ cups (420 ml) water

2½ tablespoons fish sauce

½ lime, cut into wedges, plus 2 to 3 wedges for serving

½ teaspoon paprika

¼ teaspoon ground pepper

# SHRIMP TOAST GRILLED CHEESE WITH SPICY COCONUT BROTH

## METHOD

For the shrimp toast, peel and devein the shrimp (reserve the shells to make the broth). Place about 13 shrimp in the food processor, along with the ground pork, egg white, ginger, fish sauce, and white pepper. Pulse a few times then blend for a couple minutes or until the mixture is thick and smooth. Add the remaining 5 shrimp then pulse a few times to chop them into large chunks. Transfer to an airtight container and refrigerate until ready to use.

For the spicy coconut broth, combine the reserved shrimp shells with the lemongrass, kaffir lime leaves, garlic, shallots, chiles, and galangal or ginger in a clean food processor. Pulse a few times then blend until finely chopped.

In a large pot, heat the coconut oil over medium-high heat. Add the puréed shrimp shell mixture and cook for a few minutes or until it starts to brown slightly on the sides and bottom of the pot. Add the coconut milk, water, fish sauce, lime wedges, paprika, and pepper and bring to a boil. Reduce the heat and simmer for about 30 minutes; the broth will reduce slightly. Pour the broth through a fine-mesh sieve into an airtight container, pressing on the solids to extract as much liquid as possible; discard the solids. Refrigerate until ready to use, up to 3 days.

*I didn't grow up on American grilled cheese with Campbell's tomato soup. I was never intrigued by floppy breads dipped into a bowl of watery pinkness. Call me crazy, but I crave a cube of buttery, crispy shrimp toast heightened by ginger and fish sauce and stuffed with melted provolone cheese, accompanied by a cup of spicy coconut broth infused with shrimp shells and Thai herbs. A delightful galore of different textures and flavors, an attack of all the good 'Y's—crispy, gooey, silky, salty, tangy, lemony and spicy—melding not a second earlier or later than the moment when the two components hit each other inside your mouth. Go ahead, drink Campbell's. See if I care.*

For the chili-coconut oil, in a small saucepan, combine the coconut oil and chili flakes and cook over medium heat for a couple minutes or until the chili flakes start to darken in color. Refrigerate until ready to use, up to 1 week.  Warm on low heat before use.

To make the sandwiches, generously brush one side of a slice of bread with melted butter. Spread a thin layer of the shrimp mixture on the unbuttered side then top with 3 slices of provolone or Gouda. Brush one side of a second slice of bread and place, buttered side up, on top of the cheese. Repeat to make 3 more sandwiches. Heat a heavy skillet over medium-low heat.  Place 1 to 2 sandwiches in the pan, cover the pan with foil, and cook, lowering the heat as necessary until the shrimp mixture is cooked through and the bread is golden and crispy. Repeat with the remaining sandwiches.

Divide the sandwiches among plates. Drizzle with a few drops of the chili oil, sprinkle with the chives, and serve with the spicy-coconut broth and lime wedges.

*For the chili-coconut oil*

2 tablespoons coconut oil

½ teaspoon chili flakes

Lime wedges, for serving

A Southerner at heart, photographer and stylist Beth Kirby has mastered an aesthetic that has come to define the current age of food blogging: beautiful, muted tones; deep, moody shadows; a little rustic around the edges, a little unkempt. Every scene feels lived-in, as much as the viewer wants to live in every scene. Within this new definition of perfection lies a deeper goal. For four years Kirby has pursued the notion that a blog is less a place to find information—recipes, styling tips, photography guidance—but more a place to find connection. There's a human quality to every post, insight into her life and what moves her, and like her photography, her words can be very revealing. Lately the blog has been as much travelogue and lifestyle blog as it is a resource for recipes, but the food remains central—the *raison d'être*. And the recipes mimic a cherished life: Root Vegetable Cheese Pot Pie and Herbed Biscuit Crust; Buttermilk and White Chocolate Dutch Baby; Buttermilk Beignets and Chicory Créme Pãtissiére; Jalapeño Strawberry Ice Cream; Honeysuckle Lemonade. Kirby invites the world to her table, and inspires readers to pause in order to appreciate the beauty and light in everyday life. *Local Milk* has been honored by *Saveur* Best Food Blog Awards, *Better Homes and Gardens*, *Martha Stewart Living*, The Kitchn, and many others. Kirby is a frequent contributor to magazines and other Web sites, including *Food & Wine*, *Kinfolk*, Food52, Etsy, and Lonny.

# Local Milk

**Beth Kirby**
Chattanooga, Tennessee, United States
www.localmilkblog.com

---

## Q+A

**What is the most treasured item in your kitchen?**
My collection of Japanese ceramics. The concept of *wabi-sabi* is one of the biggest inspirations for my work, and each time we visit Japan I bring a few more back.

**What is your ultimate comfort food?**
Candy. Any kind of candy. But particularly Haribo gummies of any kind and Violet Crumble candy bars. I'm an absolute sugar fiend.

**Name a utensil you can't live without.**
It's not exactly a utensil but I can't do without a digital scale. A lot of my own recipes are committed to memory by weight so I can get a bit stuck without one!

**What is your go-to breakfast?**
It changes every so often, but currently it's oat porridge with goji berries, cinnamon, brown sugar, sea salt, and bee pollen. I favor simple breakfast.

**What is your go-to cocktail?**
I don't think the Venetian Spritz leaves much room for improvement provided it has an orange twist and a green olive. Made with Campari. The Negroni is a close second.

**Who is your culinary icon?**
I have so many! I really look up to Michael Ruhlman, Anthony Bourdain, and the writer Brillat-Savarin.

# LOCAL
# MILK

# JUNIPER AND SEA SALT DARK CHOCOLATE PANNA COTTA

SERVES 6

## METHOD

Brush 6 (4-ounce / 118 ml) ramekins or molds very lightly with olive or canola oil.

In a medium saucepan, sprinkle the gelatin over 1 cup (240 ml) of the heavy cream and let bloom for 5 minutes. Set the pan over medium-low heat and cook, stirring, until the gelatin is just dissolved. Add the remaining 2 cups (480 ml) heavy cream, along with the sugar, juniper berries, and coarse sea salt and heat, stirring to dissolve the sugar, until the mixture is just about to boil and a few bubbles start to form on the sides of the pan. Remove from the heat, add the chocolate, and whisk gently until the chocolate is completely melted and incorporated. Cover and let steep for 30 minutes—you can steep the mixture longer for a stronger juniper flavor, but not too long, or it might start to set and be difficult to strain.

After steeping, pour the mixture through a fine-mesh strainer into a 4-cup (945 ml) measuring cup. Divide the mixture evenly among the prepared ramekins or molds. Chill for at least 3 hours and up to a day—if chilling for more than a few hours, cover with plastic wrap.

If you wish to unmold the panna cotta, briefly submerge the bottoms of the ramekins or molds in hot water then carefully turn the panna cotta out onto plates. Garnish with sea salt, a bit of shaved chocolate, and candied lemon, if using.

## INGREDIENTS

2 teaspoons (1 packet) powdered gelatin

3 cups (710 ml) heavy cream

1 cup (200 g) granulated sugar

2 tablespoons juniper berries, lightly crushed with a mortar and pestle

½ teaspoon coarse sea salt, plus more for garnish

1 (3½ ounce / 100 g) bar dark chocolate, finely chopped

Chocolate shavings, for garnish

Candied Meyer lemon peel (optional)

*This is my ideal holiday dessert—decadent, complex, and interesting, plus quick and so incredibly easy. It's perfect for a busy season that demands something special.*

*The recipe yields about 24 ounces of panna cotta or 6 (4-ounce / 118 ml) servings, but how you divide it up and what you serve it in is up to you—I particularly like copper molds. It's a rich dessert and a little goes a long way, so you may find you like to use smaller ramekins or molds.*

# NEW RECIPE
# WILD MUSHROOM AND CAMEMBERT STRATA

SERVES 4 TO 6

## INGREDIENTS

2 cups (480 ml) whole milk

5 large eggs

9 ounces (255 g) stale bread, cut into 1-inch (2.5 cm) cubes

1 handful (about ⅓ cup) finely chopped flat-leaf parsley leaves

1 heaping tablespoon finely chopped fresh chives

1 heaping teaspoon finely chopped fresh thyme leaves

½ teaspoon ground fennel

1½ teaspoons kosher or flaky salt

1 tablespoon olive oil

1 large shallot, cut in half lengthwise, halves cut crosswise into ¼-inch (6 mm) slices

1 large clove garlic, finely chopped

12 ounces (340 g) mixed wild mushrooms, such as oyster, maitake, lobster, chanterelle, or morels, cleaned and sliced

1 tablespoon sherry vinegar

1 tablespoon Dijon mustard

½ teaspoon freshly ground pepper

3½ ounces (100 g) cave-aged Gruyère, grated

3 ounces (85 g) Camembert, cut into small chunks

## METHOD

Preheat the oven to 375°F (190°C).

In a bowl large enough to fit all the bread, combine the milk and eggs and lightly whisk to combine. Add the bread, toss to coat, and set aside.

In a small bowl, whisk together the parsley, chives, thyme, fennel, and salt. Set aside 1 to 2 tablespoons of the herb mixture for topping the baked strata when it comes out of the oven.

In a large skillet, heat the olive oil over medium-high heat until shimmering. Add the shallot and garlic, and sauté for 2 to 3 minutes or until translucent and fragrant. Add the mushrooms, sherry vinegar, Dijon mustard, pepper, and about 2 tablespoons of the herb mixture and sauté for 4 to 5 minutes or until the mushrooms release their liquid, soften, and brown.

In a 9 x 13-inch (23 x 33 cm) or similar size baking dish, layer half the bread, mushrooms, Gruyère, and herb mixture. Top with all the Camembert. Repeat the layering with the remaining bread, mushrooms, Gruyère, and herb mixture. Bake for 40 to 60 minutes or until golden brown and puffed. Sprinkle with the reserved herb mixture and serve warm.

# MY DAILY
# SOURDOUGH
# BREAD

# My Daily Sourdough Bread

Natasa Djuric
Cerklje na Gorenjskem, Slovenia
www.mydailysourdoughbread.com

Like many food bloggers, Natasa Djuric was inspired to start *My Daily Sourdough Bread* when a health issue forced her to reconsider her diet. Digestive issues and general malaise led her doctor to recommend a gluten-free diet, but Djuric couldn't imagine life without bread. After months of research and trial and error, she realized bread made from a natural sourdough yeast might be a solution. Sourdough and sourdough-style breads have been made since the Neolithic era; they were the first leavened breads ever made. When flour and water is mixed and left out in the open air, natural yeast particles existing on the original grain or from the surrounding atmosphere begin to brew. The living yeast feasts on the sugars in wheat, essentially pre-digesting them. This process does not happen in bread made with commercial yeast. When she ate the bread made from her natural sourdough starter, Djuric discovered she didn't feel any ill effects. Djuric has been preaching her method of all-natural sourdough-starter breads since 2011 and has amassed quite a following. Her instructions for making a starter at home for the first time are easy to follow and include troubleshooting tips if something should go awry. Djuric's casual but authoritative tone, along with straightforward photographs of perfectly burnished loaves, make the blog a joy to visit daily. For the past few years she's experimented with using her starter on sweet breads as well as pastry-like baked goods. Though these breads can be more finicky to master, the step-by-step instructions make each recipe sound manageable for a lazy afternoon. In 2014 *My Daily Sourdough Bread* was awarded the best national food blog award in her home country of Slovenia.

## Q+A

**What is the most treasured item in your kitchen?**
The oven and the baking stone.

**What is your ultimate comfort food?**
Warm cinnamon rolls.

**What is your go-to cocktail?**
Limoncello.

**Who would you love to cook for?**
Researcher Brené Brown and yogi Rachel Brathen.

**Who is your culinary idol?**
Baker Ian Lowe from Apiece bakery in Tasmania.

# MOTHER SOURDOUGH STARTER

## INGREDIENTS

1 cup (120 g) whole-grain flour, such as wheat, rye, or spelt, plus more for additional feedings

½ cup (120 ml) water, plus more for additional feedings

## METHOD

*Day 1:*

To start a mother sourdough starter, in a small- to medium-sized glass jar, stir ½ cup (60 g) of the whole-grain flour with ¼ cup (60 ml) of water (note the 1:1 ratio of flour to water in weight). The mixture will be quite stiff. Cover the jar with a lid, but don't tighten it completely. Place the starter in a warm place (77 to 80°F/25 to 27°C) for 24 hours. Alternatively, place the starter in a cooler place (68°F/20°C) for 36 to 48 hours.

*Day 2 (first feeding):*

After 24 hours, you will notice the starter has risen—it may even have doubled in volume. There will be a lot of bubbles on the sides and bottom of the jar and the starter should smell sweet and pleasant. If, after 24 hours, there aren't any bubbles, leave the starter to ferment longer. If the starter is ready, use a spoon to punch it down then add ⅓ cup (40 g) of flour and 2½ tablespoons (40 ml) of water and mix well. Cover loosely and leave the starter to ferment at room temperature for 24 hours.

If there is no activity, remain patient or check the quality of the flour and the fermenting temperature, which are crucial variables in preparing a starter from scratch.

*Day 3 (second feeding):*

After another 24 hours, the starter will have again increased in volume and produced a lot of bubbles. The starter may have collapsed on itself and that is OK—it means the starter was very active and produced a lot of bubbles that couldn't hold all the weight. If the surface of the starter has dried out, scrape that part off. Use a spoon to punch the starter down then add 4 tablespoons (30 g) of the flour and 2 tablespoons (30 ml) of water and mix well. Cover loosely and leave the starter to ferment at room temperature for 24 hours.

*My following two recipes call for a homemade sourdough starter so it seemed necessary to include instructions for one here!*

*Day 4 and onward:*

If the starter is active and rises fast after each feeding, it's ready to be used in any recipe. At this point, you may want to feed it twice per day to avoid acidic notes from developing. If the starter is very sour, discard 1 to 2 tablespoons of the starter before each feeding to reduce the acidity. If the starter does not double in volume in 4 to 8 hours, keep feeding it. It should take a maximum of 5 to 7 days to make your starter active. If this is not the case, you can always add some sugar to give it a boost—try yogurt, raisin water, or kefir.

The maintainance schedule depends on how often you want to use the starter. If you bake once per week, keep your mother starter in the fridge to avoid wasting your flour for unnecessary feeding and refreshment. Every time you would like to bake, take the mother starter out of the fridge at least 12 hours before using and refresh it with 2 tablespoons of flour and 1 tablespoon of water.

**MAKES 1 LOAF**

## INGREDIENTS

*For the sourdough starter*

⅔ cup (75 g) whole-grain flour

¼ cup (75 ml) water

1 tablespoon active Mother Sourdough Starter (page 118)

*For the dough*

⅓ cup (40 g) flax seeds

1 cup plus 2 tablespoons (270 ml) water

1¾ cups (220 g) whole-grain wheat flour

2 tablespoons (40 g) sunflower seeds, toasted

⅓ cup (40 g) pumpkin seeds, toasted

1 teaspoon salt

# WHOLE WHEAT SOURDOUGH SANDWICH LOAF WITH SEEDS

## METHOD

The evening before you plan to bake the bread, prepare the starter: In a jar, combine the whole-grain wheat flour, water, and active mother starter and mix well. The batter will be stiff. Cover loosely and leave to ferment at room temperature overnight or until nicely puffed, doubled in volume, and bubbly.

In the morning, prepare the dough: In a small bowl, soak the flax seeds in 2½ tablespoons (40 ml) of the water for a few minutes until the water is completely absorbed.

In a large bowl, dissolve the sourdough starter in the remaining ¾ cup plus 2½ tablespoons (230 ml) water. Add the whole-grain flour, sunflower seeds, pumpkin seeds, flax seeds, and salt. Pay attention to the water amount—different flours absorb more or less water. The dough should be soft and moveable. If it's stiff, add 1 to 2 tablespoons more water.

Butter a 9 x 5 x 2½-inch (23 x 13 x 6 cm) loaf pan and dust it well with flour. Transfer the dough to the pan and use your fingers to flatten it a little bit. Dust the surface of the dough with flour. Cover the pan loosely with aluminum foil and let the dough rise at room temperature for 3 to 4 hours or until doubled in volume and puffed.

At least 30 minutes before the dough is ready to bake, place an empty baking dish on the bottom rack of the oven and preheat the oven to the maximum temperature.

*Hearty, healthy, fast, and easy-to-make, this seeded sandwich bread will awaken your taste buds and make your imagination blossom. Each slice is a blank canvas, offering the opportunity to dive into the art of open-faced sandwiches, or smørrebrød, as they're called in Denmark.*

*A perfectly fermented loaf will feel light in your hands; the crust will be crunchy and well browned. If the dough was under-fermented (not left to rise for enough time), the crust will be pale and the crumb tight and dense. Over-fermented dough will collapse onto itself. Tossing ice cubes into the oven creates steam while the bread bakes, contributing to the loaf's crunchy crust and lofty rise.*

When the dough is ready, throw 10 to 12 ice cubes into the baking dish to create steam and place the loaf pan in the oven. Reduce the oven temperature to 450°F (230°C) and bake for 30 minutes then reduce the heat to 400°F (200°C) and bake for another 30 minutes or until the crust is crunchy and well browned.

Remove the bread from the pan and set on a rack to cool for at least six hours or overnight. Store in sealed container for up to a week.

# SPELT BLUEBERRY SOURDOUGH SCONES

MAKES 8 TO 16 SCONES

## INGREDIENTS

*For the sourdough starter*

½ cup (50 g) whole-grain spelt flour

3 tablespoons plus 1 teaspoon (50 ml) water

1 tablespoon active Mother Sourdough Starter (page 118)

*For the scones*

2¾ cups (400 g) white spelt flour

3 tablespoons coconut sugar

Pinch of salt

½ cup plus 1 tablespoon (130 g) unsalted butter, cold and cut into small cubes

About 1 cup (230 to 240 ml) kefir

⅔ cup frozen blueberries

## METHOD

The evening before you plan to bake the scones, prepare the starter: In a jar, combine the spelt flour, water, and active mother starter and mix well. The batter will be stiff. Cover loosely and leave to ferment at room temperature overnight or until nicely puffed, doubled in volume, and bubbly.

In the morning, prepare the scone dough: In a large bowl, mix together the spelt flour, sugar, and salt. Cut the butter into the flour mixture until reduced to pea-sized lumps and completely covered in flour. In a second bowl, combine the kefir and sourdough starter and mix well. Add to the flour mixture and use your hands to gently knead just until all the ingredients come together. Pay attention to the kefir amount— different flours absorb more or less liquid, so you may not need all the kefir. Use just enough so that the dough comes together but is not too wet or too dry.

Line a baking sheet with plastic wrap. Place the dough on the plastic wrap and form into a disk, cover loosely with a second piece of plastic wrap, and let rise at room temperature for a couple hours or until puffed.

When the dough is ready, gently press the frozen blueberries into the surface. Wrap the dough in a double layer of plastic wrap and freeze for 2 hours, so that the scones will be easier to cut.

*Flaky and soft scones are a comforting treat year-round, whether with blueberries or any other fruit you choose. And sourdough? It gives these scones extra depth of flavor. The fermentation process for the scone dough may take a few hours, depending on the room temperature and the power of your starter. If you want to speed up the process, add more starter to the dough by increasing the sourdough starter ingredient quantities by one half.*

*Feel free to use different kinds of fruit in this recipe, but if using soft fruit, such as cherries, strawberries, blackberries, currants, or peaches, make sure they're frozen or you'll have difficulty pressing them into the dough.*

About 10 minutes before you take the dough out of the freezer, place a baking sheet in the oven and preheat the oven to 400°F (200°C).

Take the dough out of the freezer, remove the plastic wrap, and place on a cutting board. Cut into 16 small or 8 large scones. Remove the preheated baking sheet from the oven and carefully line with parchment paper. Arrange the scones on the lined baking sheet and bake for 20 to 25 minutes or until golden brown. Cool on a rack before serving. These scones are best eaten fresh.

For over six years, Emma Galloway has been guiding readers on an eventful life journey through the interconnected strands of her prodigious garden, adventurous kitchen, and vibrant family life. A lifelong vegetarian, avid gardener, trained chef, and mother of two, Galloway pens (gluten- and often dairy-free) recipes that are as fun to read as her prose, which can be described as inspiring, honest, and homey. The photography on *My Darling Lemon Thyme*—a nickname she uses for her daughter, and a play on the folk song "Oh My Darling, Clementine"—is as warm, colorful, and easily digestible as each story. Interspersed with mouth-watering photographs of the finished recipes are vivid images from Galloway's travels throughout Australia, New Zealand, and East Asia. Like every great cook, Galloway knows how to play with flavor, and her travels inspire new uses for ingredients like colorful curries, smoked paprika, citrus, and fresh herbs. On the sweet side, she offers the occasional raw recipe, but also knows how to indulge (think: Gluten-free Brown-Butter Spice Cake, or Flourless Chocolate Love Cake with Raspberries and Cream). *My Darling Lemon Thyme* won the Best Original Recipes category in *Saveur* Best Food Blog Awards 2014. The author of two books, Galloway is originally from New Zealand, but has lived in Perth, Western Australia, for the lifespan of her blog. She recently moved back to her childhood hometown, a development which should provide much in the way of inspiration for new gardening guides, family adventures, and memorable recipes.

# My Darling Lemon Thyme

Emma Galloway
Raglan, New Zealand
www.mydarlinglemonthyme.com

---

## Q + A

**What is the most treasured item in your kitchen?**
My high-powered blender. It gets a good workout every day.

**What is your ultimate comfort food?**
Aloo Matar with rice.

**Name a utensil you can't live without.**
My Shun Santoku knife. I love it.

**What is your go-to breakfast?**
Peanut butter and banana on homemade gluten-free sourdough bread.

**What is your go-to cocktail?**
Just a glass of apple cider. Boring, I know.

**Who is your culinary idol?**
Heidi Swanson and Yotam Ottolenghi.

# MY
# DARLING
# LEMON
# THYME

# FRIED EGG TORTILLAS WITH CUCUMBER-JALAPENO SALSA

SERVES
1

## METHOD

Combine the cucumber, jalapeño, cilantro, and lime juice in a small bowl, toss to combine, and set aside.

Warm the tortillas in a dry frying pan over medium heat until soft; keep warm.

Heat a splash of olive oil or ghee in the same pan and fry the eggs to your liking. Season to taste with salt and pepper.

Arrange the fried eggs on top of the warm tortillas. Season the salsa to taste with salt and pepper then add a few tablespoons to each tortilla. Finish with a drizzle of hot sauce and enjoy immediately.

## INGREDIENTS

1 Lebanese or Persian cucumber (or a 4-inch / 10 cm piece thin-skinned cucumber variety), seeded and finely diced

1 canned pickled jalapeño, finely diced

1 small handful fresh cilantro leaves, roughly chopped

Juice of 1 lime

2 white corn tortillas, preferably gluten-free

Olive oil or ghee, for frying

2 large eggs

Sea salt

Ground pepper

Hot sauce, such as Sriracha, for serving

*Warm tortillas topped with crispy fried eggs, spicy cucucumber salsa, and a generous drizzle of hot sauce is the kind of thing I love to make for a quick, filling lunch. The recipe makes enough for one serving, but can easily be scaled up to feed a crowd. I recommend seasoning the salsa just before serving to prevent the salt from drawing too much water from the cucumber, which will make the tortillas soggy. If you do find some liquid in the bottom of the bowl, simply drain it off. A little crumbled queso fresco or feta would be a welcome addition.*

# RHUBARB AND ROSEWATER LASSI

**SERVES 4**

## INGREDIENTS

14 ounces (400 g) trimmed rhubarb, cut into ¾-inch (2 cm) pieces

2 to 4 tablespoons unrefined cane sugar

2 cups (500 g) unsweetened yogurt

2 teaspoons high-quality rosewater, preferably organic

Ice (optional)

## METHOD

In a medium saucepan, combine the rhubarb, sugar, and a splash of water, cover and bring to a boil. Reduce the heat to medium and simmer, stirring occasionally, for 5 to 8 minutes or until the rhubarb is soft and collapsed. Remove from the heat and set aside to cool completely.

Reserve 1 to 2 tablespoons of the cooled rhubarb. In a blender, combine the rest of the rhubarb with the yogurt, rosewater, and a handful of ice, if using. Blend on high until smooth and serve immediately. Garnish the top with the reserved rhubarb, if desired.

*When the spring weather starts to warm and the rhubarb patch comes back to life after its long sleepy winter, it's the perfect time to prepare this delicately flavored lassi. Popular in India, yogurt-based drinks have long been enjoyed for their cooling properties. Adding rhubarb and a touch of floral rosewater not only creates an interesting tangy-sweet flavor profile, but it also gives the drink the most beautiful light pink hue.*

NO GOJIS,
NO GLORY

# No Gojis, No Glory

**Christine Arel**
Lammhult, Sweden
www.nogojisnoglory.com

Christine Arel's journey into blogging began when she realized her eating habits were leading not only to unwanted weight gain, but also to a general sense of unwellness. After experimenting with diets, Arel realized nothing short of a lifestyle change was going to get her back to feeling like her old self. Fast forward a couple of years: Arel isn't just talking the talk, she's also walking the walk. She says she looks and feels fantastic again thanks to an energetic life fueled by flavorful food. Her confident writing on the blog has attracted a slew of readers who follow along on her daily journey to live and eat well. Yes, goji berries make regular appearances on the blog, but it's not all superfoods and leafy greens. Arel also knows when to indulge in the likes of Roasted Red Pepper Crab Soup for her birthday or Marbled Sweet Potato Pie for the holidays. Most of the recipes are main courses, and thanks to her extensive travels (she grew up in California and lived in Hawaii, Sweden, and New York City before recently moving to Sweden) her dishes incorporate a worldwide range of flavors. The avid home cook has also mastered the art of coaxing flavors out of fish in recipes like Baked Honey-Marinated Cod and Salmon Burgers with Dill-Mustard Sauce. Alongside recipes are exercise reviews, health tips, and motivational manifestos on, for example, the benefits of yoga and the evils of yo-yo diets. It's clear readers return to *No Gojis, No Glory* because they're looking for more than a pep talk—they're looking for something authentic, and Arel delivers.

## Q+A

**What is the most treasured item in your kitchen?**
My Ninja Kitchen blender/food processor system. It's a major workhorse that doesn't take up a lot of space.

**What is your ultimate comfort food?**
French fries every time!

**Name a utensil you can't live without.**
A good wooden spoon.

**What is your go-to cocktail?**
A simple mimosa always hits the spot.

**Who would you love to cook for?**
I love to cook for friends and family. It's one of the ways I like to show my love and appreciation.

# REFRESHING MANGO-BERRY SMOOTHIE

MAKES 1

## INGREDIENTS

*For the bottom layer*

½ cup (100 g) frozen strawberries

⅓ cup (35 g) frozen blueberries

½ cup (120 ml) pure coconut water, chilled

Up to 1 tablespoon raw honey or your favorite natural sweetener (optional)

*For the top layer*

½ cup (80 g) frozen mango

⅓ cup (75 g) frozen peaches

½ cup (120 ml) pure coconut water, chilled

## METHOD

For the bottom layer, combine the strawberries, blueberries, coconut water, and honey, if using, in a blender and blend until smooth. Pour into a tall glass and freeze at least 10 minutes, while you prepare the top layer.

For the top layer, combine the mango, peaches, and coconut water in the clean blender and blend until smooth. Gently pour the mango mixture on top of the berry mixture and enjoy immediately.

*This is a fun and refreshing all-natural fruit smoothie. The mixture for each layer will be pretty thick, but this helps with the layering effect. Both smoothies thin out pretty quickly, so be sure to serve this right away. If you'd prefer a more liquid smoothie, just combine all the ingredients with more coconut water and blend until you reach your desired consistency.*

# SUPREME GREEN QUINOA CRUST PIZZA

SERVES 2

## METHOD

Preheat the oven to 500°F (260°C). Line a round 10-inch (25 cm) cake pan with parchment paper.

For the quinoa pizza crust, thoroughly rinse the soaked quinoa under cold running water to remove any bitterness then drain off excess water. Transfer to a high-powered blender, along with the water, eggs, avocado or grapeseed oil, baking powder, oregano, and salt and blend until smooth. Scrape the mixture into the prepared pan. Bake for 25 minutes or until golden brown.

While the crust is baking, prepare the cashew cheese: In a high-powered blender, combine the cashews, lemon juice, and pepper and blend until smooth.

For the toppings, in a large skillet, heat the avocado or grapeseed oil over medium heat and sauté the broccolini or broccoli rabe and asparagus for 2 minutes; season lightly with salt. Add the garlic and sauté for another 3 minutes, or until the vegetables are bright and tender. Remove from the heat.

When crust is finished baking, spread the cashew cheese on top of the crust. Arrange the broccolini or broccoli rabe, asparagus, and artichoke hearts on top. Bake for another 5 to 10 minutes or until the cheese and toppings are heated through. Serve immediately.

## INGREDIENTS

*For the quinoa pizza crust*

1 cup (170 g) uncooked quinoa, soaked in water for 6 to 8 hours

½ cup (120 ml) water

2 large eggs

1 teaspoon avocado or grapeseed oil

½ teaspoon baking powder

½ teaspoon dried oregano

½ teaspoon fine sea salt

*For the cashew cheese*

1 cup (150 g) unsalted cashews

3 tablespoons freshly squeezed lemon juice

¼ teaspoon ground pepper

*Toppings*

1½ tablespoons avocado or grapeseed oil

5 ounces (140 g) broccolini or broccoli rabe, trimmed

4 ounces (115 g) asparagus, trimmed

Fine sea salt

2 large cloves garlic, minced

2 canned artichoke hearts, roughly chopped

*This healthy yet undeniably satisfying pizza has a nutritious quinoa crust and is topped with nutrient-rich greens. The cashew cheese is a delicious dairy-free pizza topping, but you can substitute any sort of cheese you like.*

Now here's a story: Astroparticle physics student starts a food blog. Before long, she drops out of graduate school to study the pastry arts. She works in bakeries. She continues to blog. She misses physics, quits job as pastry chef, and becomes a high school science teacher. Meanwhile, she keeps this affair, this pastry affair, orbiting her life—on her blog. Kristin Rosenau's focus on desserts sets her blog apart from many others, but her sensibilities in the kitchen transcend sugar, flour, and eggs. Her practical science background informs a precision most home bakers lack, but she knows when to pull out a comforting mess of crumb cakes and baked puddings. Photography is juxtaposed with thoughtful quotations, and the blog is traditional in the sense that Rosenau shares her everyday life with longtime readers who cheer her on, engage in lively discussions over the merits of puff pastry from scratch, and offer their own tips. Though Rosenau favors making doughs from scratch, she does suggest helpful shortcuts for the busy home baker. Photographs of more difficult processes—éclair dough, pastry cream, lemon curd—demonstrate texture and consistency and give novice cooks something to rely on. Plus, everything on *Pastry Affair* just looks too good not to make, from the Swedish Tea Ring to the Caramel Apple Crumble Pie to a Dulce de Leche Cake with Swiss Meringue Icing. A finalist in *Saveur*'s Best Food Blog awards, *Pastry Affair* has been featured in *Bon Appetit*, the *Guardian*, and *Food & Wine* magazine.

# Pastry Affair

**Kristin Rosenau**
Minneapolis, Minnesota, United States
www.pastryaffair.com

---

## Q+A

**What is the most treasured item in your kitchen?**
A coffee mug.

**What is your ultimate comfort food?**
Vegetable soup.

**What is your go-to breakfast?**
Hot quinoa porridge.

**What is your go-to cocktail?**
A lime margarita with a sugared rim.

**Who would you love to cook for?**
Friends and family.

**Who is your culinary icon?**
Julia Child.

# PASTRY AFFAIR

# CHOCOLATE CACAO NIB BANANA BREAD

**MAKES 1 LOAF**

## METHOD

Preheat the oven to 350°F (180°C). Butter a 9 x 5-inch (23 x 13 cm) loaf pan.

In a medium bowl, use a fork to mash 3 of the bananas until smooth. Set aside.

In a separate medium bowl, whisk together the flour, cocoa powder, baking soda, baking powder, salt, and cacao nibs.

In a large bowl, beat together the butter and brown sugar with a mixer until light and fluffy. Add the eggs, 1 at a time, incorporating each egg before adding the next, and beat for 2 to 3 minutes or until creamy. Add the vanilla extract and the mashed bananas and beat until fully incorporated. Fold in the flour mixture, then add the milk and mix until uniform.

Scrape the batter into the buttered pan. Cut the remaining banana in half lengthwise and press both halves into the top of the loaf. Sprinkle with additional cacao nibs and bake for 55 to 65 minutes or until a skewer inserted in the center comes out clean. Let the loaf cool for 10 minutes before taking it out of the pan. Set on a rack to cool completely. Wrapped tightly, the loaf will keep for several days at room temperature.

## INGREDIENTS

4 large ripe bananas, peeled

1 ½ cups (190 g) all-purpose flour

½ cup (45 gm) cocoa powder

1 teaspoon baking soda

1 teaspoon baking powder

½ teaspoon salt

½ cup (60 g) cacao nibs, plus more for sprinkling

½ cup (115 g) unsalted butter, at room temperature

¾ cup (150 g) packed light brown sugar

2 large eggs

1 teaspoon vanilla extract

½ cup (120 ml) whole milk

*I decided long ago that it wasn't possible to have too many banana bread recipes. With this particular loaf, I wanted to create a version that's somewhere between breakfast and dessert. Cocoa powder lends rich chocolate notes, while a sprinkling of cacao nibs provide interesting flavor and texture. The loaf relies largely on the natural sugars in the bananas for its sweetness. If desired, the cacao nibs can be substituted with chocolate chips for a more decadent treat. Serve with a tall glass of milk.*

## NEW RECIPE
# PLUM ALMOND CRUMBLE

## INGREDIENTS

*For the plum filling*

2 pounds (900 g) ripe black plums, pitted and sliced

⅓ cup (65 g) packed light brown sugar

⅓ cup (40 g) all-purpose flour

1 teaspoon vanilla extract

½ teaspoon ground cinnamon

Pinch of ground nutmeg

*For the almond crumble topping*

3 tablespoons unsalted butter

¼ cup (50 g) packed light brown sugar

½ cup (50 g) ground almonds

½ cup (45 g) rolled oats

¼ cup (30 g) all-purpose flour

⅛ teaspoon salt

Vanilla ice cream or whipped cream, for serving

## METHOD

Preheat the oven to 375°F (190°C).

For the plum filling, in a large bowl, combine the plums, brown sugar, flour, vanilla, cinnamon, and nutmeg and gently toss to evenly coat the fruit. Spread the mixture in the bottom of a 9-inch (23 cm) deep-dish pie plate or a cast iron pan. Set aside.

For the almond crumble topping, in a medium bowl, combine the butter and brown sugar and beat with a mixer for several minutes or until light and uniform. Add the almonds, oats, flour, and salt and stir by hand until fully incorporated. Using your fingers, break the mixture into crumbles and sprinkle it evenly over the plums.

Bake for 40 to 50 minutes or until the top is golden and the plums are bubbling. Transfer to a rack to cool. Serve warm or at room temperature, topped with vanilla ice cream or whipped cream.

*Summer brings an abundance of fresh fruit and since I can't resist filling my basket at the market, crumbles have become one of my favorite ways to feature the season's amazing bounty. For this crumble, plums are sliced and mixed with just a hint of cinnamon and nutmeg to add warmth, while ground almonds and oats are sprinkled on top to create an irresistibly crumbly texture. Served with whipped cream or vanilla ice cream, this crumble is a true celebration of summer, and perfect for long summer nights.*

# Ren Behan

St. Albans, England, United Kingdom
www.renbehan.com

Ren Behan recently expanded her blog to include recipes and tutorials. She also teaches classes on lifestyle blogging and is involved in the wider food blogging community. All of which might explain why reading *Ren Behan* is such a pleasant way to spend a few hours on a lazy afternoon, clicking around for recipe inspiration. After a stint as a lawyer, Behan went on to study journalism and food styling, and started her first blog in 2010 as a way to preserve the Polish recipes she grew up on. Cut to today, and Behan is a powerhouse blogger who reviews products and restaurants, hosts giveaways, and has a cookbook on the way. Based in England, Behan has easy access to ingredients from Poland. Her three young children vet her recipes, so they're kid-friendly, too. Eastern European traditions inform Behan's stories and recipes, but she's modernized them for the everyday cook. Think: Beetroot and Kale Soup with Almond Crumble; Blueberry Pierogi with Cinnamon Cream; and her mama's *Bigos*. Recipes lean toward hearty—enriched breads, meaty stews, thick soups—but Behan features fresh spring and summer produce when it's in season. Come December, ideas abound for gifts like Rum Pot, Pomegranate and Vanilla Vodka, and Polish Spiced Christmas Cookies. Behan also contributes to *JamieOliver.com*, the Good Food Channel, Great British Chefs, and LoveFood. Her first book on modern Polish cooking hits shelves in the United Kingdom in 2017.

---

## Q+A

**What is the most treasured item in your kitchen?**
My cookbook collection. I have a huge bookcase in my kitchen because I believe that cookbooks should be used and covered in sticky fingerprints.

**What is your ultimate comfort food?**
Roast chicken served with macaroni and cheese.

**What is your go-to breakfast?**
Sourdough rye with cream cheese, drizzled with raw honey.

**What is your go-to cocktail?**
I love the combination of vodka, ginger beer, and Grand Marnier. Or a Polish martini, made with two types of vodka and cloudy apple juice.

**Who is your culinary idol?**
British food writer Diana Henry, who writes so passionately about food and always inspires and opens up a whole new world of flavors through her writing.

# WILD MUSHROOM SOUP WITH KASHA

**SERVES 6 TO 8**

## INGREDIENTS

½ cup (40 g) dried porcini mushrooms

1 cup (240 ml) hot water

2 carrots, peeled and halved lengthwise

2 ribs celery, trimmed

1 onion, peeled and halved

2 to 3 allspice berries

1 fresh bay leaf

2 quarts (2 L) plus ¼ cup (60 ml) cold water

1 cube mushroom or vegetable bouillon

1 tablespoon butter

1 pound (450 g) wild, porcini, or cultivated brown, mushrooms, trimmed and chopped

1 teaspoon freshly squeezed lemon juice

2 teaspoons cornstarch

1 cup (240 ml) heavy cream

2 cups (100 g) cooked kasha

Sea salt

Ground pepper

2 tablespoons finely chopped fresh flat-leaf parsley, for garnish

Rye bread, for serving

## METHOD

In a small bowl, combine the dried porcini mushrooms with the hot water and soak for ten minutes or until softened.

While the mushrooms are soaking, start the soup: In a large pot, combine the carrots, celery, onion, allspice berries, bay leaf, and the 2 quarts (2 L) cold water. Crumble in the bouillon cube and bring to a gentle boil. Reduce the heat and simmer for 20 minutes.

Strain the soaked porcini mushrooms through a fine-mesh strainer and pour the soaking liquid into the soup. Finely chop the rehydrated mushrooms and add them to the soup. Remove the carrots, celery, onion, allspice berries, and bay leaf.

In a large sauté pan, melt the butter over medium heat. Add the wild or cultivated mushrooms and sauté for five minutes or until softened. Stir in the lemon juice then add the mushrooms to the soup.

In a small bowl, whisk the cornstarch with the remaining ¼ cup (60 ml) cold water then add to the soup. Increase the heat, and return to a rolling boil. Stir in the heavy cream and add the cooked kasha. Season to taste with salt and pepper, garnish with the parsley, and serve with the rye bread.

*Polish mushroom soup is very often made with wild forest mushrooms, as mushroom hunting is still undertaken with great pleasure across Poland. Outside of mushroom season, you can use dried forest mushrooms with a handful of fresh mushrooms thrown in. I like adding beautiful winter chanterelles (kurki in Polish) but fresh porcini or cultivated brown mushrooms work well, too. My mother adores mushroom hunting, just as her mother did, and this recipe never fails to bring me back to my childhood.*

*To the finished soup, I add cooked kasha, which is a type of grain. You can use either buckwheat groats or cracked barley groats. If you can't find kasha, use rice instead.*

SERVES
12

## INGREDIENTS

*For the vodka-soaked cherries*

2 cups (450 g) pitted cherries

½ cup (100 g) granulated sugar

1 cup (240 ml) vodka

*For the cheesecake base*

2 cups (260 g) all-purpose flour

½ cup (115 g) unsalted butter

½ cup (100 g) granulated sugar

2 large egg yolks

*For the cheesecake filling*

3 cups (675 g) twaróg, full-fat cream cheese, curd cheese, or farmer's cheese

1 cup (200 g) granulated sugar

½ cup (115 g) unsalted butter

5 large eggs, whites and yolks separated

1 teaspoon vanilla bean paste or extract

1 tablespoon all-purpose flour or cornstarch

# BAKED VANILLA CHEESECAKE WITH VODKA-SOAKED CHERRIES

## METHOD

For the vodka-soaked cherries, combine the cherries, sugar, and vodka in a sterilized jar and let marinate for at least 2 days or up to 1 week. Strain the cherries, reserving the cherry-infused vodka to enjoy separately.

Preheat the oven to 350°F (180°C). Butter a 13 x 9-inch (33 x 23 cm), 2½-inch (6 cm) deep baking pan and line with parchment paper.

For the cheesecake base, combine the flour, butter, sugar, and egg yolks in a food processor and pulse until well combined. Transfer the mixture to the lined baking pan and press into a flat, even layer. Prick the pastry with a fork a few times then bake for 15 minutes or until golden. Set aside to cool. Maintain oven temperature.

For the cheesecake filling, combine the twaróg or cream cheese, sugar, butter, egg yolks, and vanilla in a large bowl and whisk until well combined. Stir in the flour or cornstarch.

In a clean medium bowl, whip the egg whites until stiff peaks form. Carefully fold into the cheesecake mixture then pour the batter over the cooled pastry base. Bake for 45 minutes or until golden on top but still a little wobbly. Switch off the oven, open the door, and leave the cheesecake to cool inside the oven for 30 minutes.

*Baked cheesecakes are common in Eastern Europe, and in Poland, baked cheesecake is called sernik. This is a simple and traditional recipe, served with vodka-soaked cherries. The cherries can be made up to a week in advance and have the added bonus of producing cherry-infused vodka. Start the cherries at least 2 days before you plan to serve the cheesecake, and note that the cheesecake itself has to chill in the refrigerator overnight.*

*The best cheese to use for sernik is twaróg, but you can also use full-fat cream cheese, curd cheese, or farmer's cheese. If the cheese isn't smooth, push it through a fine-mesh sieve before using.*

Take the cheesecake out of the oven, let it cool completely at room temperature, then place in the refrigerator to chill overnight.

Cut the cheesecake into squares, and serve with vodka-soaked cherries on the side.

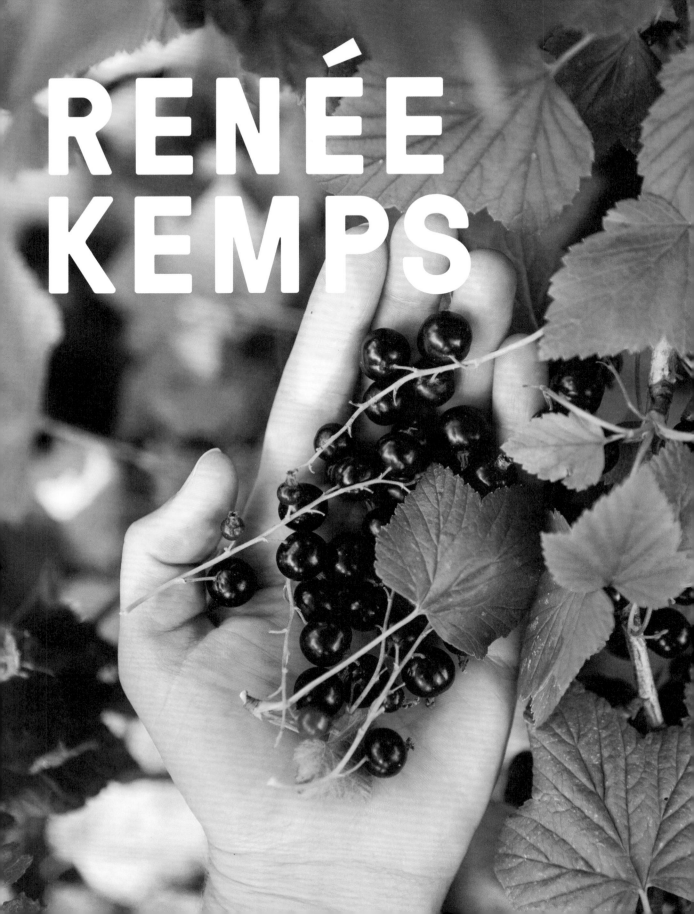

# Renée Kemps

London, United Kingdom
www.reneekemps.com

Renée Kemps grew up on an old farm, picking apples and making pie, and her adult life aspires to a similar level of pastoral perfection, though she recently moved to London from Amsterdam. Fortunately, the New Nordic Kitchen Manifesto, developed by chefs and restaurateurs, supports Kemps's personal mission as well as that of her eponymous blog. *Renée Kemps* is as much recipe journal as daily diary. Readers follow along so as to vicariously live the clean, calm, beautiful life Kemps portrays. Minimalist photography and Scandinavian-inspired design play a major part in the site's appeal, and make it a pleasure to look at even if you have no interest in food. But the food is the focus, like the deep crimson of her Roasted Bone Broth Tomato and Bean Soup; the velvety white of a Spring Greens and Herb Salad with Fresh Goat Cheese; the sienna brown nooks of her Sourdough Spelt Waffles. Kemps has an eye for visual composition and she employs it well. In between recipe posts are travelogues for cities throughout Europe. The tastes and sights and smells of these travels—into Tokyo, through Iceland, and in Ireland—inform recipes once Kemps is back home. Green Asparagus and Tarragon Soup is as vivid as the Irish countryside; Whole Wheat, Cinnamon, and Blood Orange Hot Cross Buns would be lovely with afternoon high tea. Kemps contributes to publications including Food52, Life & Thyme, and *Jamie* magazine, and her blog is a winner of *Saveur*'s Best Food Blog Awards 2015 for Best Photography.

---

## Q+A

**What is your ultimate comfort food?**
Creamy Burrata, smoked or roasted fresh, seasonal vegetables, good quality olive oil, and lots of fresh herbs.

**Name a utensil you can't live without.**
A Microplane grater.

**What is your go-to breakfast?**
Sourdough French toast.

**What is your go-to cocktail?**
Early: greyhound. Late: espresso martini.

**Who is your culinary idol?**
Dan Barber.

# SMOKED BEETS WITH PESTO, BURRATA, PEACH, AND DUKKAH

SERVES 2

## INGREDIENTS

2 small red beets

2 tablespoons olive oil, plus more for serving

Sea salt

Ground pepper

2 tablespoons basil pesto

1 ball Burrata cheese

1 peach, very thinly sliced

Fresh mint leaves

Red shiso leaves (optional)

*For the dukkah*

2 tablespoons crushed hazelnuts

1 tablespoon white sesame seeds

1 tablespoon coriander seeds

½ tablespoon cumin seeds

Sea salt, to taste

Ground pepper, to taste

## METHOD

Preheat the oven to 475°F (250°C).

Pierce the beets with a fork, rub with olive oil, and sprinkle with sea salt and black pepper. Place the beets on a baking sheet and roast, rotating the pan a few times, for 50 to 70 minutes, or until completely cooked through and slightly charred. Let cool slightly.

While the beets are cooking, make the dukkah: In a small dry skillet over medium heat, toast the hazelnuts until golden and fragrant. Repeat with the sesame seeds, coriander, and, cumin, toasting each one individually to avoid burning. Use a mortar and pestle to lightly grind and crush the nuts and spices together. Season with salt and pepper.

Spread the pesto on 2 plates. Cut the beets into wedges and arrange them on top of the pesto. Split the Burrata in half and place one half on each plate. Divide the peaches, mint, and shiso leaves, if using, between the plates. Drizzle with olive oil, sprinkle with the dukkah, and serve.

*Whenever there's a beet dish on the menu at a restaurant, I order it. Give me beets, Burrata, good olive oil, fresh herbs, and a bottle of wine, and I'm yours. I love everything about beets—their texture, color, flavor, and versatility. I especially adore beets blistered and sweet; when you smoke or roast them, their skins loosen and crisp up a little, while the insides turn soft and become just a little bit sweeter—it's a to-die-for combination.*

*For this recipe I roast the beets, but they are also delicious smoked.*

# NEW RECIPE
# LITTLE BLACK CURRANT CAKES

MAKES
12 CAKES

## METHOD

Preheat the oven to 350°F (180°C). Butter and flour a 12-cup muffin pan.

In a large bowl, whisk together the flour, baking powder, and salt.

In the bowl of a stand mixer fitted with the paddle attachment, beat the butter and granulated sugar on medium-high until light and fluffy, about 3 minutes. Add the eggs, 1 at a time, incorporating each egg before adding the next one, and beat for 2 to 3 minutes or until creamy. Scrape down the sides of the bowl as needed. Add the orange zest, vanilla paste, and almond liqueur and mix on low until combined. With the mixer on low, add the flour mixture a third at a time, alternating with the milk. Scrape down the sides of the bowl and mix until just combined.

Scrape the batter into the prepared pan, pouring ¼ cup (60 ml) of the batter into each cup. Arrange 5 to 8 black currants on top of each and lightly sprinkle with raw cane sugar. Bake for 15 to 18 minutes or until the tops are golden brown and a skewer inserted in the center of the cakes comes out clean. Let the cakes cool slightly before removing from the pans. Serve plain or dusted with confectioners' sugar, sprinkled with more currants, and topped with vanilla ice cream.

## INGREDIENTS

2 cups (260 g) all-purpose flour

½ teaspoon baking powder

¼ teaspoon sea salt

¾ cup (170 g) unsalted butter, at room temperature

1 cup (200 g) granulated sugar

3 large eggs, at room temperature

Zest of 1 large orange

½ teaspoon vanilla bean paste

Splash of almond liqueur

¼ cup (60 ml) dairy or non-dairy milk of choice

1 cup (180 g) black currants, plus more for serving

Raw cane sugar, for sprinkling

Confectioners' sugar and vanilla ice cream, for serving

*Every summer, sometimes in June, sometimes in July, the black currants in my parents' garden are ready for harvest. Soft, big, and bursting with juices—they're almost so heavy they'll fall to the ground as soon as they catch a breeze. We make liters of black currant syrup—stocking up, so we can enjoy black currant lemonade all year long—but there are still so many black currants left over. I developed this recipe out of a desire to find another good use for our bounty. Aside from the fruit, these cakes feature a few of the ingredients we like at home—a little booze, a generous hit of orange zest. They're a sweet little treat yet have a bit of tanginess. Best of all, these are some of the easiest cakes you'll ever make, perfect for whipping up when you're overloaded with fruit.*

Julia Gartland's eye for light and space and color is so well tuned that she can make bruised bananas look beautiful. So it should come as no surprise that she studied photography in school, and only began her life as a food blogger when digestive problems forced her to look closely at her diet and eating habits. *Sassy Kitchen* is all about gluten-free living, with a focus on whole foods and options for dairy-free, vegetarian, and vegan alternatives. Though she blogs from Brooklyn, Gartland has embraced a California ethos and a minimalist, Scandinavian aesthetic. Interspersed with recipes like Kale Caesar Salad with Roasted and Spiced Chickpeas and Turmeric and Candied Ginger Ice Cream are gorgeous product guides and design-focused round-ups. Recipes read like photo essays, and change with the seasons. A post on Butterscotch Chocolate Chunk Sea Salt Cookies is accompanied by woodsy still lifes featuring flannel backdrops, while the sun-drenched photos of wildflowers and wooden bins overflowing with ripe, fuzzy peaches for a Classic Summer Peach Pie post bring to mind golden reveries of farmers' markets. Throughout, Gartland experiments with various gluten-free flours and flavors, adding helpful notes and suggested tips for novices and experts alike. Gartland keeps her recipe intros light, friendly, and focused on the food and season, which makes the blog a welcome respite from an otherwise noisy Internet. *Sassy Kitchen* was twice a *Saveur* Best Food Blog Award finalist and has been covered in dozens of publications, including Food52, *Elle*, and *Harper's Bazaar*.

# Sassy Kitchen

**Julia Gartland**
Brooklyn, New York, United States
www.sassy-kitchen.com

---

## Q+A

**What is the most treasured item in your kitchen?**
My vintage spoons, ceramics collection, and Staub pans.

**What is your ultimate comfort food?**
Tacos and hippie bowls. Anything that reminds me of California and feeds my soul.

**What is your go-to cocktail?**
In the summer, I love Campari sodas, Negronis, and a great rosé. In the colder months, anything with bourbon or a nice bold Italian red wine.

**What is your go-to breakfast?**
On busy days, a green smoothie or avocado toast with a soft egg. On less busy days, I love frittatas and sorghum pancakes.

**Who would you love to cook for?**
I love cooking for strangers. There's something about making a meal for someone that I find incredibly intimate.

**Who is your culinary idol?**
Julia Child, Nigella Lawson, and anyone with passion and a bit of sass in the kitchen.

# SASSY
# KITCHEN

# THYME AND SUMAC CHICKPEA SOCCA WITH ARUGULA, PISTACHIO, AND FETA SALAD

SERVES 4

## INGREDIENTS

*For the socca*

1 cup (90 g) chickpea flour

2 teaspoons ground sumac

1 teaspoon sea salt

1 teaspoon ground pepper

1 cup (240 ml) lukewarm water

4 tablespoons (60 ml) olive oil, plus more as needed

1 medium sweet onion, chopped

1 clove garlic, finely chopped

3 tablespoons fresh thyme leaves, plus more to taste

Zest and juice of ½ lemon

*For the salad*

3 large handfuls baby arugula

½ fennel bulb, shaved

½ red onion, thinly sliced

⅓ cup (50 g) pistachios, lightly toasted and roughly chopped

2 ounces (60 g) high-quality sheep's milk feta, crumbled

Flaky sea salt

Ground pepper

## METHOD

For the socca, in a large bowl, whisk together the chickpea flour, sumac, salt, and pepper. Slowly whisk in the lukewarm water—mind that you eliminate all lumps. Whisk in 2 tablespoons of the olive oil then fold in the onion, garlic, thyme, and lemon zest and juice. Let the batter sit and thicken for at least 15 minutes or up to 12 hours. It should have the consistency of heavy cream.

Preheat the oven to 450°F (230°C).

Coat a 8-inch (20 cm) skillet or cast iron pan with the remaining 2 tablespoons olive oil and place it in the hot oven to preheat for about 10 minutes or until very hot. Carefully remove the hot pan from the oven and pour in the socca batter, spreading it evenly in the pan. Season to taste with salt, pepper, and thyme then bake for 12 to 15 minutes or until the edges are golden brown and firm. If the socca appears dry while baking or afterwards, drizzle a little olive oil over the top. Let cool for 15 to 20 minutes.

For the salad, in a large bowl, toss together the arugula, fennel, red onion, and pistachios.

*For as long as I can remember, socca has been one of my favorite go-to meals. Somewhere between a delicious pan bread and pizza with a twist, socca are made almost entirely of chickpea flour, so they're naturally gluten, grain, and dairy-free.*

*In colder months, it's nice to add wintry herbs like rosemary and thyme, but I also love to use sumac for it's lemony brightness. After too many gray months, I'm in need of a change of pace from broth-y chicken soups and this is just the right pick-me-up. Top socca with some lovely greens and you'll swear it's spring.*

For the dressing, in a small mason jar, combine the lemon juice, vinegar, mustard, and garlic. Gradually add the olive oil in a thin, steady stream, whisking, until the dressing reaches the desired thickness. Cover the jar and shake well to emulsify the dressing.

Drizzle the dressing over the salad, sprinkle with the feta, and season to taste with flaky sea salt and pepper. Cut the socca into wedges and divide among 4 plates. Top each plate with a handful of salad and serve.

*For the lemon-Dijon dressing*

2 teaspoons freshly squeezed lemon juice

1 teaspoon red wine vinegar

1 teaspoon whole-grain Dijon mustard

1 clove garlic, finely chopped

2 tablespoons olive oil, plus more as needed

# SORGHUM DOUGHNUTS WITH STRAWBERRY-RHUBARB GLAZE

MAKES
2 DOZEN
DOUGHNUTS

## INGREDIENTS

1 cup (100 g) ground almonds

1 cup (135 g) sorghum flour

1 teaspoon baking powder

½ teaspoon ground cinnamon

½ teaspoon ground cardamom

½ teaspoon sea salt

½ cup (120 ml) maple syrup

6 tablespoons (90 ml) extra-virgin coconut oil

3 large eggs

2 teaspoons vanilla extract

Zest of 1 lemon

*For the glaze*

1 heaping cup (115 g) chopped rhubarb

1¼ cups (200 g) quartered strawberries

1 tablespoon unsalted butter

Pinch of sea salt

¼ cup (60 ml) maple syrup

2 tablespoons heavy cream or coconut cream

2 teaspoons freshly squeezed lemon juice

## METHOD

Preheat the oven to 325°F (160°C). Butter a mini doughnut pan.

For the doughnuts, in a large bowl, whisk together the ground almonds, sorghum flour, baking powder, cinnamon, cardamom, and salt. In a medium bowl, whisk together the maple syrup, coconut oil, eggs, vanilla extract, and lemon zest. Add to the almond-sorghum mixture and fold in with a rubber spatula until well combined.

Carefully scrape the batter into a pastry bag or use a large resealable plastic bag and cut ½ inch (12 mm) off one of the corners. Pipe half the batter into the prepared pan, filling each cup about three-quarters full. Bake for exactly 10 minutes then let cool for 5 minutes. Transfer the doughnuts to a rack to cool then butter the pan, fill the cups with the remaining batter, and bake the rest of the doughnuts.

For the glaze, in a medium saucepan, cook the rhubarb, strawberries, and butter over medium-low heat, stirring occasionally, for 10 to 12 minutes or until the rhubarb is soft but still maintains its shape. Remove from the heat and let cool.

Transfer the cooled fruit mixture to a food processor, add the sea salt, maple syrup, heavy cream or coconut cream, and the lemon juice and pulse until completely smooth. Transfer the glaze to a shallow bowl and chill in the refrigerator for 20 minutes.

Once the glaze has cooled, dip each doughnut into the glaze, gently tilting the doughnut with a circular motion to evenly distribute the glaze over one side. Serve immediately.

*There is nothing quite like those brief but miraculous few weeks when rhubarb and strawberries are in season at the same time. Together they're refreshingly tart and sweet, a culinary match made in heaven. That's what makes these strawberry and rhubarb glazed doughnuts the perfect spring-into-summer treat, ideal for a crowd and a guaranteed showstopper for any weekend brunch.*

# SOUTHERN SOUFFLÉ

# Southern Soufflé

**Erika Council**
Atlanta, Georgia, United States
www.southernsouffle.com

Emboldened by her life experiences and those of her family, writer and photographer Erika Council reaches into the depths of her heritage when drafting passionate posts that address what some might see as uncomfortable issues for a food blog. Racial inequality, police brutality, poverty, and cultural diversity are just some of the topics Erika tackles. Yet *Southern Soufflé* is a casual, comfortable space that also happens to be honest and sometimes even raw. Though the recipes are the focus of each post, Council weaves a narrative into every introduction, adding a soulful element. On *Southern Soufflé*, recipes like Salted Benne Seed Brittle, Classic Buttermilk Cake, and Cornbread Calas stand out not only because of Council's natural-light photography but because of the ease with which she describes each step, like a mother bird nudging her chicks into the kitchen. Not every step of a recipe is photographed, but the important ones—showing the texture of the dough, the viscosity of the batter, and the final shade of golden brown on that biscuit— are all that a confident cook needs. Recipes like Duck Fat Beignets, White Peach Cobbler Muffins, Drunken Jelly Doughnut Milkshakes, and Banana Cream French Toast read like something from the cover of a food magazine. A self-described computer software nerd and self-taught cook, Council grew up in North Carolina and now lives (and cooks) in Atlanta. *Southern Soufflé* is a member of the Southern Foodways Alliance; their mission is to study and explore the traditional and emerging foodways of the South.

## Q+A

**What is the most treasured item in your kitchen?**
An old cast iron skillet. I have over fifty of them but this one belonged to my grandmother and she got it from her mother. I can only imagine how many buttermilk biscuits have risen in it.

**What is your ultimate comfort food?**
Biscuits. I make them constantly and in all types of variations.

**What is your go-to breakfast?**
A bowl of yogurt topped with granola and whatever fruit I have on hand.

**Who would you love to cook for?**
I would've loved to cook for Edna Lewis.

**Who is your culinary idol?**
Mildred Cotton Council, my grandmother. Her restaurant in Chapel Hill, NC, has been open for over three decades.

SERVES 6

## INGREDIENTS

*For the slaw*

2 cups (200 g) shredded green cabbage

2 cups (200 g) shredded red cabbage

1½ cups (265 g) shucked fresh corn kernels

1 cup (125 g) peeled, julienned carrots

1 red bell pepper, cored, seeded, and thinly sliced

1 jalapeño, seeded and minced

½ cup (25 g) roughly chopped fresh cilantro leaves

⅓ cup (80 ml) olive oil

Juice of 1 lemon

1 clove garlic, finely chopped

1 teaspoon kosher salt

¼ teaspoon ground pepper

¼ teaspoon ground red pepper

*For the tomatoes*

½ cup (120 ml) buttermilk

1 cup (130 g) all-purpose flour

½ cup (75 g) coarse yellow cornmeal

2 teaspoons coarse salt

¼ teaspoon ground pepper

4 green tomatoes, cut into ½-inch (12 mm) thick slices

½ cup (120 ml) peanut oil, for frying

# BUTTERMILK FRIED GREEN TOMATOES WITH SPICY-SWEET CORN SLAW

## METHOD

For the slaw, combine the green and red cabbage, corn kernels, carrots, bell pepper, jalapeño, and cilantro in a large bowl and toss to combine.

In a small bowl, whisk together the olive oil, lemon juice, garlic, salt, and pepper. Pour over the cabbage mixture and toss to combine. Cover and refrigerate while you fry the tomatoes.

For the tomatoes, pour the buttermilk into a shallow bowl. In a second shallow bowl, whisk together the flour, cornmeal, salt, and pepper.

Dip the tomato slices, 1 at a time, in the buttermilk then dredge them in the flour mixture—mind that they're evenly coated—and tap gently to remove any excess flour mixture.

Heat 1 inch (2.5 cm) of peanut oil in a large, heavy skillet over medium-high heat. When the oil is hot enough, use tongs to carefully dip 3 to 4 tomato slices in the oil—mind that they're not touching each other. Fry for 2 minutes or until the tomatoes are golden brown then flip over and fry the other side for 2 minutes or until golden brown. Transfer to paper towels to drain. Repeat with the remaining tomato slices—mind that the oil stays hot enough.

To serve, arrange the fried green tomatoes on plates and top with slaw.

*Fried green tomatoes are a mainstay in Southern cuisine. When I was growing up, they were always dipped in buttermilk, fried, and then topped with a red tomato, cucumber, and vinegar "salad." Here, I've adapted that version, by swapping in a simple slaw that gets a kick from jalapeño and a sweet crunch from fresh corn.*

# CHEDDAR AND THYME CORNMEAL HOECAKES

MAKES
6 CAKES

## METHOD

Combine the cornmeal and salt in a medium bowl. While stirring constantly, slowly add the boiling water. Add the cheddar and thyme and stir until well incorporated. Let stand for about 2 minutes.

In a large cast iron skillet, heat the bacon fat over medium-high heat. Working in batches, drop 2 tablespoon dollops of the batter into the skillet and pat gently into flat circles, roughly 4 inches (10 cm) in diameter. Cook about 2 minutes per side or until golden brown and crisp. Transfer to paper towels to drain, and repeat with the remaining batter, adding more bacon fat if necessary. Serve warm.

## INGREDIENTS

1 cup (195 g) fine yellow cornmeal

½ teaspoon salt

¾ cup (180 ml) boiling water

¼ cup (25 g) shredded sharp cheddar

2 tablespoons chopped fresh thyme leaves

2 tablespoons rendered bacon fat, plus more as needed (from 4 to 5 slices bacon)

*Think of a savory cornbread flapjack with fresh thyme and sharp cheddar and you have a close idea of how insanely wonderful these hoecakes are. Traditionally, hoecakes are made with white cornmeal and hot water, using a method that closely resembles that of hot water cornbread, then they're drizzled with sorghum or molasses and served hot.*

Unapologetic and indulgent with a rock 'n' roll sensibility, Emily Von Euw (Em, to her readers) sidesteps the frivolity that sometimes befalls food blogs and just gets real. Her spunky prose and strong ethical compass inform recipes as varied as Blueberry Hemp Smoothies, Raw Pizza with Spinach Pesto and Marinated Vegetables, and an unrepentantly gooey-looking Deep Dish Caramel Apple Pie. Every post is illustrated with lush, highly saturated photography. Von Euw's gratitude and mindfulness inspire omnivorous readers to try whole food ingredients they might not otherwise consider, while revealing posts about her love life and personal adventures keep readers coming back for more of her emotionally "raw" stories. Informative write-ups on wellness and body products add even more to the blog's spirited appeal. Still in school, the young blogger says she woke up one day and "decided to be vegan" just like that. The epiphany was not marked by any major life event, but led her down a thoughtful road where "being vegan simply means caring about others." The author of three cookbooks, most recently *The Rawsome Vegan Cookbook*, Von Euw lives with her parents who are now "99 percent vegan" just outside Vancouver, British Columbia. *This Rawsome Vegan Life* won first place in the Vegan Woman's 2013 Vegan Food Blog Guide, and has been named among the top 50 raw food blogs by the Institute for the Psychology of Eating.

# This Rawsome Vegan Life

Emily Von Euw
Vancouver, British Columbia, Canada
www.thisrawsomeveganlife.com

=== **Q + A** ===

**What is the most treasured item in your kitchen?**
My Vitamix blender. I use it every day—usually two or three times—to make smoothies, nut milks, soups, sauces, banana ice cream, and chocolate.

**Name a utensil you can't live without.**
A good rubber spatula. Way less food waste.

**What is your go-to breakfast?**
A giant smoothie and/or a bowl of oatmeal with coconut sugar, almond butter, vanilla, and cinnamon.

**Who would you love to cook for?**
Myself! Can't lie. When I make myself happy, it feels great.

**Who is your culinary idol?**
Laura Miller (author of *Raw. Vegan. Not Gross.*) is pretty hilarious and incredibly gorgeous.

# THIS
# RAWSOME
# VEGAN
# LIFE

# RAW CARROT CAKE WITH CASHEW CREAM FROSTING

SERVES 8 TO 12

## METHOD

For the frosting, in a high-powered blender, combine the cashews, maple syrup, coconut oil, and lemon juice and blend until smooth. If the mixture is too thick, add water, 1 tablespoon at a time, to loosen. Transfer to a bowl and set aside.

For the carrot cake, in a food processor, combine the carrots, oat or buckwheat flour, dates, pineapple, coconut, and cinnamon and pulse until the mixture forms a rough, moist dough and holds its shape.

To assemble the carrot cake, press half the cake mixture into the bottom of a 6-inch (15 cm) springform pan. Spread about ⅓ of the frosting on top then place the pan in the freezer and freeze until the frosting is firm. Press the remaining cake mixture into the pan on top of the frosting. Remove the sides of the springform pan and spread the remaining frosting all over the top and sides of the cake. Alternatively, refrigerate the cake overnight then remove the sides of the springform pan and frost. The cake can be made and refrigerated, covered, 1 to 2 days in advance.

## INGREDIENTS

*For the cashew cream frosting*

2 cups (300 g) cashews, soaked in water for 4 hours then rinsed and drained

⅓ cup (80 ml) maple syrup

2 tablespoons liquid coconut oil

1 to 2 tablespoons freshly squeezed lemon juice

Water, as needed

*For the carrot cake*

2 large peeled carrots, cut into chunks

1½ cups (135 g) oat or buckwheat flour

1 cup (175 g) pitted dates

1 cup (175 g) dried pineapple

½ cup (30 g) dessicated coconut

½ teaspoon ground cinnamon

*This is the most popular recipe on my blog and with good reason. It's everything you want a carrot cake to be, without all the refined and processed ingredients. I love cake, and I love it even more when it's good for my body.*

*Soaked nuts are easier for your body to digest, so try not to skip that step!*

SERVES
8-12

# EASY SUPERFOOD CHOCOLATE BAR BITES

## INGREDIENTS

¼ cup (60 ml) coconut oil

2 heaping tablespoons maple syrup

2 heaping tablespoons cacao powder

¼ teaspoon vanilla powder or extract

¼ teaspoon red chile powder (optional)

Pinch of Himalayan salt

2 tablespoons goji berries

1 teaspoon raw white sesame seeds

1 teaspoon chia seeds

1 tablespoon cacao nibs

## METHOD

In a small pot, melt the coconut oil over low heat. Take the pot off the heat then add the maple syrup, cacao powder, vanilla powder or extract, chile powder, if using, and salt and whisk until the mixture is completely smooth. Pour into a medium-sized chocolate mold coated lightly with coconut oil or onto a medium-sized baking sheet lined with aluminum foil, spreading the mixture evenly and making sure it doesn't spill over the edges.  Sprinkle with the goji berries, sesame seeds, chia seeds, and cacao nibs then refrigerate or freeze until hard, cut into pieces, and enjoy. Store the chocolate in the freezer for up to 5 days, transferring to the fridge an hour before serving.

*I love chocolate—I eat it almost every day. This is one of my go-to recipes, because I can whip it up in just a few minutes and it's nutritious, sweet, and satisfying.*

*Cacao is cocoa powder that goes through a more gentle refining process in order to maintain the highest level of nutrition. Its flavor is slightly sharper, spicier, and more flowery than cocoa. You can use cacao powder and cocoa powder interchangeably.*

# THREE LITTLE HALVES

# Three Little Halves

**Aleksandra Mojsilovic**
New York, New York, United States
www.threelittlehalves.com

Aleksandra Mojsilovic is a data science researcher who spends her free time writing stories about food and family and life on *Three Little Halves*. The name of the blog comes from a Serbian poem in which a warrior has a habit of cutting his enemies into "three halves," an odd and memorable unit of measurement, and one which comes in handy in the kitchen. It's both playful and practical and far more jarring than just saying "thirds." Similarly, Mojsilovic's prose and photography arrests the eyes. Her language dances between formality and the chitter-chatter of children. The imagery on the blog is a blend of maximalist montages, elaborate collages, aerial photographs that depict fantastical scenes, and minimalist plays on color, texture, and form. This is not photo direction or styling, this is art. And though the images might make each recipe seem a touch unreal, Mojsilovic's easy writing takes everything back to the hearth. Recipe inspiration comes mostly from international sources—Eastern Europe, Southeast Asia, and Italy factor heavily in dishes like Eduard Sacher Torte, Old Fashioned Serbian Apple Pita, Sri Lankan Kale Mallung, and Pumpkin Lasagne "Bolognese"—though American fare makes appearances as well, as in Rustic Biscuits with Candied Bacon and Jalapeño. The success of *Three Little Halves* is a testament to Mojsilovic's tenacity. Though work and family life keep her busy, she always finds a bit of time to blog. *Three Little Halves* is the winner of IACP's Best Narrative Culinary Blog 2016 and was a finalist for Best Original Recipes in the *Saveur* Best Food Blog Awards 2014.

## Q+A

**What is the most treasured item in your kitchen?**
My mom's book of recipes.

**What is your go-to breakfast?**
Two cups of Assam tea with milk and honey.

**What is your go-to cocktail?**
Martini. Gin and dry vermouth in 6:1 ratio, stirred, with three olives. Definitely not dirty.

**Who would you love to cook for?**
Jeffrey Steingarten.

**Who is your culinary idol?**
All the anonymous cooks of this world, our mothers and grandmothers, the street vendors, the pit masters, the tea blenders, the bakers—I learn from them every single day.

# READER FAVORITE
# FRAGRANT COD AND WHITE ALE CURRY

**SERVES 4**

## INGREDIENTS

1 teaspoon coriander seeds

2 tablespoons vegetable oil

1 small shallot, finely chopped

1 clove garlic, finely chopped

½ large stalk lemongrass, finely chopped with tough outer layer removed

1-inch (2.5 cm) piece fresh ginger, peeled and cut into slices

1 to 1 ½ cups (240 to 350 ml) coconut milk

1 tablespoon Thai red curry paste

1 tablespoon fish sauce

1 teaspoon freshly grated lime zest

6 cardamom pods, lightly crushed with a mortar and pestle

8 fresh basil leaves, plus more for garnish

4 fresh large curry leaves (optional)

2 (12-ounce / 355 ml) bottles wheat beer, such as Hoegaarden

Salt

1 pound (455 g) cod filets, cut into strips 2 inches (5 cm) wide

1 tablespoon freshly squeezed lime juice

## METHOD

In a dry, heavy skillet over medium heat, toast the coriander seeds for a few minutes or until fragrant.

In a medium saucepan, heat the vegetable oil over medium heat. Add the shallot and garlic and sauté for about 2 minutes or until soft. Add the lemongrass, ginger, coconut milk, curry paste, fish sauce, lime zest, cardamom, basil, curry leaves, if using, and the toasted coriander. Reduce the heat to low and simmer until very thick and reduced by two-thirds.

While the curry sauce is simmering, cook the fish: Bring the beer to a boil in a large saucepan. Season to taste with salt then reduce the heat to low so the beer is simmering. Add the cod in a single layer, making sure it's completely submerged, and poach for 8 minutes or until the flesh is flaky and opaque. Divide the fish among 4 bowls. Reserve 1½ cups (350 ml) of the beer and discard the rest.

Stir the reserved beer into the reduced curry sauce. Pour through a fine-mesh sieve into a large bowl then return the sauce to the saucepan and simmer over medium-low heat for 5 to 6 minutes to heat the sauce and allow the flavors to combine. Stir in the lime juice and pour the sauce over the fish. Garnish with basil leaves and serve.

*Beer and curry is a match made in heaven. This curry is light, creamy, and smooth, and beautifully fragrant thanks to the lime, basil, lemongrass, coriander, and cardamom. White ale and a touch of curry paste make for a sunny yellow sauce and contribute to this dish's good looks. Be sure to have plenty of rice on hand to sop up all the great curry sauce—it's pretty difficult to resist.*

*Fresh curry leaves can be difficult to source, so don't stress if you can't find them. When I happen to have them on hand, I throw them in for an extra brownie point of goodness, but I often make this recipe without them and it's still super satisfying.*

ARAL
SEA

Bokhara

ARABIAN

SEA

INDIAN

OCEAN

Miles
250        500        750

900        800        1200
Kilometres

# ALONG THE SILK ROAD COCKTAIL SHORTBREADS

**MAKES 20 SHORTBREADS**

## METHOD

In a large bowl, use an electric mixer to beat the butter and turbinado sugar until pale, creamy, and well combined.

Sift together the flour, salt and your choice of spice mixture. Add to the butter mixture and mix on low until the ingredients come together and a crumbly dough forms. Transfer the dough to a work surface and use your hands to gently gather and compress the mixture together. Pat the dough into a log about 1¼ inches (3 cm) in diameter. Wrap the log in plastic wrap and refrigerate until firm, at least 4 hours, but preferably overnight.

Preheat the oven to 325°F (160°C), preferably on convection setting. If you do not have convection setting, preheat the oven to 350°F (175°C). Line a large baking sheet with parchment paper.

Cut the dough into slices ¼-inch (6 mm) thick and arrange on the lined baking sheet. If you would like, prick the tops of the shortbreads with a fork, or use a knife to create a line pattern. Bake for about 20 minutes or until the shortbreads are golden but haven't started to brown around the edges. Let the shortbreads cool on the baking sheet for 5 minutes, then carefully slide the parchment onto a wire rack and let the shortbreads cool completely. The shortbreads can be kept in an airtight container for about a week.

*For the shortbread*

½ cup (115 g) unsalted butter, at room temperature

¼ cup (50 g) turbinado sugar

1¼ cups (160 g) all-purpose flour

½ teaspoon kosher salt

*For the western route*

½ teaspoon ground ginger

½ teaspoon ground coriander

½ teaspoon ground fennel

½ teaspoon ground white pepper

¼ teaspoon ground cumin

*For the eastern route*

½ teaspoon Chinese five-spice powder

½ teaspoon chipotle chile powder

½ teaspoon smoked paprika

¼ teaspoon cayenne pepper

*Opening a spice jar is magical and adding a dash of spice to a simple dish feels like letting the genie out of the bottle. Whether it's a touch of cumin, a pinch of coriander, or a hint of fennel, if we combine spices with a few high-quality ingredients, suddenly we find ourselves on a journey along the Silk Road, remembering that once upon a time, spices were tightly guarded and more precious than gold. They created civilizations, destroyed empires, and led to the discovery of new continents.*

*This recipe lets you follow your own spice journey. Choose the route— eastern or western—that suits your palate or mood. Or, double the recipe, make a batch of each spice mixture, and explore both flavor profiles. The shortbread dough needs to be made at least four hours ahead, so allow enough time for it to chill in the refrigerator.*

# Twigg Studios

Aimee Twigger
Devon, England, United Kingdom
www.twiggstudios.com

Aimee Twigger's gorgeously styled photography, fit for a high-end home magazine, keeps fans coming back to scroll through her latest creations. They're usually cakes. But not just any cakes: Only fanciful, towering, fantastically decorated cakes are featured, from a hummingbird cake wearing a floral crown to a dulce de leche cake made from a marble loaf and glazed with a blood orange icing. Twigger's strength is in taking a familiar dessert and applying a new set of flavors to it, like Masala Chai Cake with Persimmon Stem Ginger Jam and Maple Candied Walnuts, or Vegan Cake with Avocado Lime Coconut Cream Frosting. It's no surprise Twigger's idol is *The Great British Bake Off* judge and proper lady Mary Berry. When she's not making cakes she's likely making something else that's equally sweet: a rhubarb pie with a lattice that looks like a window in a Frank Lloyd Wright house; a towering Pavlova; or an inventive Banana Cream Bostock with Sesame Halva and Almond Cream. There are introductory level recipes as well, like Buckwheat Brown Butter Banana Brownies and Carrot Cake Waffles that promise to take everyday delights to a new level. But fans come back for Twigger's fantastical creations, and even sign up to attend retreats in which she teaches budding bloggers how to style magazine-quality photography—lighting, angles, props and all. Twigger is the author of two cookbooks, *Aimee's Perfect Bakes*, and *Love, Aimee X*.

## Q+A

**What is the most treasured item in your kitchen?**
My KitchenAid mixer.

**What is your ultimate comfort food?**
I have a sweet tooth so I love chocolate.

**Name the utensil you can't live without?**
A silicone spatula. I use it all the time, it's so handy.

**What is your go-to breakfast?**
I love yogurt and granola with honey.

**What is your go-to cocktail?**
Cosmopolitan.

**Who is your culinary idol?**
Mary Berry—she is the queen of baking.

TWIGG
STUDIOS

# HUMMINGBIRD CAKE WITH PINEAPPLE-LIME JAM AND COCONUT FROSTING

**SERVES 8**

## INGREDIENTS

*For the jam*

1 pineapple, cored and cut into chunks (reserve small uncut section for pineapple flower decoration; optional)

1½ cups (350 ml) fresh pineapple juice

Zest of 2 limes

1¼ cups (250 g) granulated sugar

*For the sponge cake*

½ cup plus 1 tablespoon (125 g) unsalted butter, at room temperature

1 cup plus 1 tablespoon (235 g) muscovado sugar

2 large eggs

2 ripe bananas, mashed with a fork

¼ cup plus 2 tablespoons (90 g) canned crushed pineapple

1 teaspoon vanilla extract

2 cups (250 g) all-purpose flour

2 teaspoons baking powder

1 teaspoon salt

3 tablespoons desiccated coconut, plus more for decorating

½ cup (50 g) pecans, chopped

## METHOD

For the jam, in a large, heavy pan over medium heat, combine the pineapple chunks, pineapple juice, and lime zest. Cook for 45 minutes or until the pineapple is soft. Add the granulated sugar and cook for 25 minutes or until the sugar has dissolved and the mixture begins to thicken. Transfer to a food processor and pulse a few times to break up the pineapple. Return the mixture to the pan and cook for 10 minutes or until reduced, thick, and jam-like. Let cool slightly then pour into a sterilized jar. The jam can be made ahead and kept in the refrigerator for up to 1 month.

Preheat the oven to 350°F (180°C). Butter 2 (4- to 6-inch / 11- to 15 cm) round cake pans and line the bottoms with parchment paper.

For the cake, in a large bowl, use an electric mixer to beat the butter and muscovado sugar for a few minutes or until light and fluffy. Add the eggs, 1 at a time, incorporating each egg before adding the next one, and beat for 2 to 3 minutes or until creamy.

In a small bowl, stir together the banana, pineapple, and vanilla then add to the butter-sugar mixture and stir to combine.

In a medium bowl, sift together the flour, baking powder, and salt. Add the coconut and the ½ cup chopped pecans and toss to combine. Add to the butter-sugar mixture and fold until combined. Scrape the batter into the prepared pans and bake for 40 to 50 minutes or until golden and well risen. If you insert a skewer in the center, it should come out clean. Let the cakes cool for at least 15 minutes before taking them out of the pans and transferring onto a wire rack to cool completely.

*This is one of my favorite desserts. It features a banana-pineapple sponge cake that's studded with coconut and pecans, plus a layer of tangy pineapple-lime jam and creamy coconut frosting.*

For the frosting, in a large bowl, use an electric mixer to whip the heavy or double cream, mascarpone, coconut cream, and confectioners' sugar for a few minutes or until soft peaks form. Add the honey and whip for a few minutes or until the frosting is thick and creamy.

To assemble the hummingbird cake, spread 4 tablespoons of the jam on top of 1 of the sponge cakes then carefully add a layer of frosting and place the second sponge cake on top. Spread the remaining frosting all over the top and sides of the cake and sprinkle with some desiccated coconut on all sides.

To make the pineapple flower decorations, slice the reserved pineapple thinly with a mandolin. Bake the slices on a baking sheet in a 210°F (100°C) oven, turning every 30 minutes, for about 2 hours or until dried. Bend the pineapple slices into flower shapes and place them in a muffin pan to set.

To make the candied pecans, in a small sauce pan, bring the maple syrup to a rolling boil. Add the 1 cup pecans, and swirl around in the pan to coat. Carefully pour the mixture onto a parchment paper-lined baking sheet, spreading it evenly. Let cool until hard.

Garnish the cake with the pineapple flowers and candied pecans, if using, and enjoy.

### For the frosting

1¼ cups (300 ml) heavy or double cream

1 cup (250 g) mascarpone

⅓ cup plus 2 tablespoons (100 ml) coconut cream

5 tablespoons confectioners' sugar

4 tablespoons honey

### For the pineapple flowers and candied pecans (optional)

Reserved pineapple (from above)

5 tablespoons maple syrup

1 cup (100 g) pecans

**SERVES 5**

# LEMON AND POPPY SEED GRANOLA

## INGREDIENTS

2 cups (200 g) rolled oats

½ cup (50 g) pecans

½ cup (50 g) walnuts

½ cup (50 g) cashews

4 tablespoons sliced almonds

4 tablespoons sunflower seeds

4 tablespoons pumpkin seeds

2 tablespoons poppy seeds

2 tablespoons brown sugar (optional)

Zest and juice of 1 large lemon

5 tablespoons (75 ml) honey

¼ cup (60 ml) olive oil

1 teaspoon bee pollen (optional)

1 tablespoon marigold petals (optional)

## METHOD

Preheat the oven to 340°F (170°C). Line a baking sheet with parchment paper.

In a large bowl, toss together the oats, all of the nuts, seeds, the brown sugar, if using, and the lemon zest. In a small bowl, stir together the honey, olive oil, and lemon juice. Add to the oat mixture and stir until completely coated. Spread the mixture out on the lined baking sheet and bake, stirring every 10 minutes—mind that you stir around the edges—for about 35 minutes or until golden. Let cool then stir in the marigold petals and bee pollen, if using, and enjoy. Keep in an airtight container for up to 2 weeks.

*I love making granola, because it's just so easy to throw together. When I make it myself, I usually don't use strict measurements for the nuts and seeds—it's just a handful of each—but I've included measurements here for those who prefer to be more precise. My favorite way to eat this granola is with some honey-sweetened Greek yogurt.*

# THE WOKS
# OF LIFE

# The Woks of Life

Bill, Judy, Sarah, and Kaitlin Leung
New York, New York, United States
www.thewoksoflife.com

Bill, Judy, Sarah, and Kaitlin Leung are a family of food lovers. They started their blog when Bill and Judy moved to China in 2011, leaving their two college-aged daughters, Sarah and Kaitlin, behind. The Web site was a way for them to all connect, and for Bill and Judy to share their culinary heritage with their daughters, who grew up with Chinese cuisine but hadn't yet learned to make many of the traditional dishes they loved to eat. Meanwhile, Sarah and Kaitlin shared their own takes on American, French, Japanese, and Spanish cuisine, demonstrating how America's melting pot embraces each generation. A couple of years ago Bill and Judy moved back to the United States and now the family gathers together every few weeks to cook up a feast. The recipes jump off the page, familiar at once to Americans and those who grew up around Chinese cuisine: Cumin Lamb is a popular Xinjiang dish, while Mall Chicken Teriyaki recalls those savory toothpicked samples served in front of mall food courts from Nevada to New Jersey. Vivid photography accompanies each post, but it's really the stories and confident yet casual writing that keep readers reading and encourages cooks to start cooking. The best part of *The Woks of Life* might be the easy-to-understand recipe index, organized by ingredient, meal, cuisine, or occasion. The section on Chinese takeout might be the most fun; it's where the family dives into the histories behind common takeout dishes like Mongolian Beef (not actually Mongolian) or Peking pork chops (sweet and sour pork chops; not a traditional dish from Beijing) and provides recipes that go beyond everyday takeout fare. *The Woks of Life* won Best Special Interest Blog in the *Saveur* Best Food Blog Awards 2015.

---

## Q+A

**What is the most treasured item in your kitchen?**
Bill's father's old cleaver. It has his initials carved into the handle, and it's still sharp!

**What is your ultimate comfort food?**
Anything in the window of a great Cantonese takeout restaurant—crispy roast pork, *char siu*, or soy sauce chicken. That fluorescent-lit, grease-splattered window is a little piece of home.

**Name a utensil you can't live without.**
Chopsticks. They do triple duty as a fork, a knife, or even a steaming rack in a pinch.

**What is your go-to breakfast?**
No one has ever said no to scallion pancakes.

**Who is your culinary idol?**
We all really enjoyed watching the Two Fat Ladies—they were never ones to cower in the face of the butter needed to move from good to great.

# 15-MINUTE COCONUT-CURRY NOODLE SOUP

SERVES 2 TO 4

## INGREDIENTS

2 tablespoons vegetable or canola oil

3 tablespoons Thai red curry paste

3 cloves garlic, chopped

1 tablespoon freshly grated ginger

8 ounces (225g) skinless, boneless chicken breasts or thighs, thinly sliced

4 cups (950 ml) chicken broth

1 cup (240 ml) water

⅔ cup (160 ml) coconut milk

2 tablespoons fish sauce

Salt

6 ounces (170 g) dried rice vermicelli noodles

Juice of 1 lime

Red onions, thinly sliced, for garnish

Fresh red chilies, seeded and finely chopped, for garnish

Fresh cilantro leaves, roughly chopped, for garnish

Green onions, thinly sliced, for garnish

## METHOD

In a large pot, heat the oil over medium heat. Add the curry paste, garlic, and ginger and sauté for 5 minutes or until fragrant. Add the chicken and sauté for 2 minutes or just until the chicken turns opaque. Add the chicken broth, water, coconut milk, and fish sauce and bring to a boil. Season to taste with salt if needed; if the broth is too salty, add a bit of water.

Divide the vermicelli noodles among bowls and pour the boiling soup on top—the noodles will be ready in 1 to 2 minutes. Alternatively, add the noodles to the boiling broth, cook them for 30 seconds, then divide among serving bowls. Add a squeeze of lime juice and your garnishes and serve immediately.

*We're ardent fans of absolutely any dish having to do with noodles and hot soup, and this is one of the best—and easiest—noodle soups you'll ever make. As the name suggests, it takes only 15 minutes to pull together. And yet despite the speediness of the recipe, this soup has amazingly complex flavor. The richness of the coconut milk, the spicy zing of the curry paste, the tangy bite of the lime, and the funky awesomeness of the fish sauce culminate in the perfect bowl of noodles.*

*Another win? Unlike other noodle soups, this is a one-pot dish. Using thin rice noodles is key—you can just throw them into the pot at the end and serve the soup almost immediately, or put the dried noodles in a bowl and pour the hot broth on top.*

# STEAMED PORK AND BOK CHOY BUNS

MAKES
16 BUNS

## INGREDIENTS

*For the buns*

3 cups (390 g) all-purpose flour

½ teaspoon baking powder

¾ cup (180 ml) hot water

¼ cup (60 ml) milk

1 tablespoon granulated sugar

1½ teaspoons active dry yeast

1 tablespoon vegetable oil

*For the filling*

1 pound (455 g) boneless pork shoulder

⅓ cup (80 ml) vegetable oil

2 tablespoons water

1½ tablespoons soy sauce

1½ tablespoons granulated sugar

1 tablespoon Shaoxing rice wine (or dry sherry)

2 teaspoons toasted sesame oil

2 teaspoons salt

2 pounds (910 g) baby bok choy

## METHOD

For the buns, in the bowl of a stand mixer fitted with the dough hook attachment, whisk together the flour and baking powder. In a small bowl, combine the hot water, milk, and sugar and stir until the sugar is completely dissolved. Add the yeast and let stand for 10 minutes.

With the mixer on low, slowly add the yeast mixture to the flour mixture. Add the vegetable oil and with the mixer on medium-low, knead the dough for about 10 minutes or until smooth. Alternatively, knead the dough by hand for 15 to 20 minutes. Cover with a damp towel and let rise in a warm place for 1 hour.

For the filling, use 2 sharp knives to chop the pork with quick up and down motions until it resembles ground meat—mind that it should take 5 to 10 minutes to fully chop the pork. Transfer the pork to a large bowl, add the vegetable oil, water, soy sauce, sugar, rice wine or sherry, sesame oil, and salt and stir to combine. Set aside.

Bring a large pot of water to a boil. Working in batches, blanch the bok choy for 10 seconds then immediately transfer the greens to an ice bath to stop the cooking process. Finely chop the bok choy, add to the pork mixture, and stir well to combine.

To assemble the buns, cut out 16 (3-inch/7.5 cm) squares of parchment paper. Knead the dough by hand for 5 minutes, divide it into 16 equal pieces, and cover with a damp towel. Use a rolling pin to roll out each piece of dough into a circle 4 inches (10 cm) in diameter, with the

*These steamed buns take a little time to put together, but the results are worth it. The secret to a great filling is to chop the pork by hand, an old-school method that's been around for generations.*

*We're steaming the buns, but you can also pan-fry them: Place the buns in an oiled cast iron pan over medium-high heat and cook until the bottoms brown then add about ½ inch (1 cm) of water to the pan, cover, and cook until the water evaporates.*

*If you don't have a multi-level steamer, you can use a bamboo steamer set in a wok. Place the steamer in the wok and fill the wok with enough water to reach ½ inch (1 cm) up the sides of the bamboo steamer. Steam the buns in batches and be sure to watch the steamer as the buns cook to ensure that the water level stays consistent and the steamer does not burn.*

center slightly thicker than the outer edges. Add 2½ tablespoons of filling to the center of a dough circle, and wrap the dough around the filling, pleating the edges repeatedly until the filling is completely enclosed and the bun is sealed. Put the bun on a parchment square and place it on a steaming rack. Repeat with the remaining filling and dough until all the buns are assembled and in the steamer. Allow the buns to rest in a warm place for 15 minutes.

To cook the buns, add 2 inches (5 cm) of cold water to the bottom of the steamer and set the steamer over medium-high heat for 15 minutes. Remove from the heat and let the buns continue to steam for 5 more minutes. Serve immediately.

Though home for Virpi Mikkonen is Helsinki, Finland, her food blog—which has a distinct natural foods bent, thanks to Mikkonen's training as a health coach—features recipes inspired by cuisines from around the globe. With little fanfare she breaks down flavors, textures, and ingredients, swiftly announcing new gluten-, yeast-, and dairy-free recipes as if they were as crave-inducing as a traditional Neapolitan pie. Thanks to bright, airy photography that spotlights the food, wholesome recipes are celebrated and appear as easy to prepare (or even simpler) as the original. Sometimes special ingredients are called for, but Mikkonen addresses each and offers suggestions on where and how to find them. Like many health-focused food bloggers, Mikkonen also dabbles in DIY beauty, but it doesn't distract from her recipes. A kids' section playfully presents vegan treats like coconut popsicles, grape sorbet, and (yes, vegan!) chocolate pudding. Thanks to a former career in magazines, she knows how to pair words with photographs, edit recipes, and create dishes that appeal to a wide audience. Her Sea Salt Toffee Candies, Dairy-Free Banana Coconut Yogurt, and smoothies—from cardamom raspberry to pistachio fig—all look and sound like the perfect thing to make on a weekend morning, whether it's Helsinki, Brooklyn, Sacramento, Indianapolis, or Pittsburgh outside your door. Her newest book, *N'ice Cream* (about vegan ice cream) and *It's a Pleasure* (about healthy sweet treats) are in bookstores as of 2016. Mikkonen is also the author of several shorter digital cookbooks, including a smoothie guide and one focused on vegan dessert. *Vanelja* is written in both Finnish and English.

# Vanelja

**Virpi Mikkonen**
Helsinki, Finland
www.vanelja.com

---
## Q+A
---

**What is the most treasured item in your kitchen?**
An old Indian glass cabinet where I keep all my props, old plates, bowls, cutlery, and so on.

**What is your ultimate comfort food?**
It has to be healthy vegan ice creams! One of my favorite combos is simply frozen banana, almond butter, and raw cocoa powder.

**What is your go-to cocktail?**
Nature's own cocktails, such as coconut water, birch sap, and spring water.

**Who would you love to cook for?**
My parents. I see them too rarely as they live so far away.

**Who is your culinary idol?**
Taline Gabrielian has a brilliant style and I share the same vision with her about cooking wholesome food free of gluten, dairy, and refined sugar.

VANELJA

# STRACCIATELLA CHOCOLATE CAKE

SERVES
6

## METHOD

Preheat the oven to 350°F (180°C) and set a rack in the middle of the oven. Oil a 7-inch (18 cm) round cake pan with coconut oil and line the bottom with parchment paper.

For the cake, in a medium bowl, whisk together the coconut flour, almond flour, cacao powder, baking powder, psyllium husk, and vanilla powder or extract. In a large bowl, beat the eggs with the coconut palm syrup or honey and coconut sugar with an electric mixer for 1 to 2 minutes or until the mixture is light and fluffy. Add the flour mixture and stir to combine. Stir in the oat milk. Let the dough thicken for 5 minutes.

Pour the batter into the prepared pan and bake for 35 to 40 minutes or until a skewer inserted into the center of the cake comes out clean. Let the cake cool completely in the pan on a baking rack before taking it out of the pan—if necessary, use a knife to cut around the edges of the cake to release it from the pan. When the cake has cooled, slice it horizontally into 2 layers.

While the cake is baking, make the stracciatella filling: Remove the cans of coconut milk from the refrigerator, open, and scoop all the solid white coconut cream into a bowl. Use an electric mixer to beat the coconut cream until fluffy. Add the coconut palm syrup or honey, vanilla powder or extract, and cacao nibs and beat just to combine. If the mixture is too runny, refrigerate for about 15 minutes or until the texture resembles whipped cream.

To assemble the cake, spread the almond butter on top of the bottom cake layer then top with half of the stracciatella filling. Arrange the second cake layer on top and spread the remaining stracciatella filling all over the top of the cake. Sprinkle grated raw chocolate on top of the cake and serve. Store the cake in the refrigerator and enjoy within 4 days.

*This amazing cake combines layers of deep and luscious chocolate cake with creamy vanilla-scented frosting and crunchy cacao nibs. Plus, it's both grain- and dairy-free, whereas Stracciatella is typically a milk-based gelato.*
*Raw cacao powder, used in this recipe, is made by cold-pressing unroast-ed cocoa beans, whereas cocoa powder is roasted at high temperatures.*

## INGREDIENTS

*For the cake*

Coconut oil, for greasing the pan

½ cup (50 g) coconut flour

½ cup (50 g) almond flour

½ cup (60 g) raw cacao powder

2 teaspoons baking powder

1 teaspoon psyllium husk*

1 teaspoon vanilla powder or extract

6 large eggs, preferably organic and free-range

5 tablespoons coconut palm syrup or honey

5 tablespoons coconut palm sugar

½ cup (120 ml) oat milk

*Psyllium husk, a common ingredient in gluten-free baking, is made from the seed of the plant *Plantar ovata*. It improves texture and helps the cake to rise.

*For the stracciatella filling*

2 (13.5-ounce / 400 ml) cans full-fat coconut milk, refrigerated overnight

1 tablespoon coconut palm syrup or honey

½ teaspoon vanilla powder or extract

5 tablespoons raw cacao nibs

*For assembling the cake*

5 tablespoons almond butter

Grated raw chocolate

**NEW RECIPE**

# DREAMY BLUEBERRY BREAKFAST BARS

MAKES 6 BARS

## INGREDIENTS

*For the crust*

1 cup (100 g) rolled oats, preferably gluten-free

½ cup (75 g) white sesame seeds

½ cup (70 g) almonds

7 soft fresh dates, pitted

2 tablespoons coconut oil, melted

1 teaspoon vanilla extract

½ teaspoon ground cardamom

Pinch of sea salt

*For the filling*

½ cup (70 g) fresh or frozen blueberries

1 (13.5-ounce / 400 ml) can full-fat coconut milk, chilled

1 ripe banana

½ cup (70 g) cashews

4 tablespoons coconut oil, melted

3 to 4 tablespoons maple syrup or coconut syrup

1 tablespoon freshly squeezed lemon juice

1 teaspoon vanilla extract

Fresh or frozen blueberries and shredded coconut, for the topping

## METHOD

Line an 8-inch (20 cm) square baking pan with parchment paper, allowing 1 to 2 inches (2.5 to 5 cm) of parchment to hang over the sides for easy removal.

For the crust, combine the oats, sesame seeds, almonds, dates, coconut oil, vanilla, cardamom, and salt in a blender and blend for 30 seconds or until a moldable dough forms. Season to taste with more cardamom or vanilla. Press the crust firmly and evenly onto the bottom of the lined baking pan. Set aside.

For the filling, in a clean blender, purée the blueberries until smooth. Measure 2 tablespoons of the puréed blueberries and set aside. Add the coconut milk, banana, cashews, coconut oil, maple or coconut syrup, lemon juice, and vanilla to the blender and purée for 30 seconds or until the mixture is smooth. Season to taste with more syrup or vanilla. Pour over the crust in the pan, spreading it evenly. Drop small spoonfuls of the reserved blueberry purée on top and use a toothpick to swirl it into the filling. Sprinkle the blueberries and shredded coconut on top then freeze the bars overnight.

The next day, remove the bars from the freezer and thaw for about 20 minutes. Use the parchment overhang to lift the block from the pan, cut it into 6 small bars, and serve. Store in an airtight container in the freezer or refrigerator for up to 3 days.

*Like a smoothie and granola combined, these lovely blueberry bars are the perfect way to start the day—they make a healthy and delicious week-end breakfast.*

# Index